NUMEROLOGY EASY GUIDE FOR BEGINNERS

Discover Who You Are, Learn About Your Life and Uncover Your Destiny Through Numerology, Astrology, Numbers, And Tarot Reading

Michelle Northrup

© Copyright 2019 by Michelle Northrup - All rights reserved.

This content is provided with the sole purpose of providing relevant information on a specific topic for which every reasonable effort has been made to ensure that it is both accurate and reasonable. Nevertheless, by purchasing this content you consent to the fact that the author, as well as the publisher, are in no way experts on the topics contained herein, regardless of any claims as such that may be made within. As such, any suggestions or recommendations that are made within are done so purely for entertainment value. It is recommended that you always consult a professional prior to undertaking any of the advice or techniques discussed within.

This is a legally binding declaration that is considered both valid and fair by both the Committee of Publishers Association and the American Bar Association and should be considered as legally binding within the United States.

The reproduction, transmission, and duplication of any of the content found herein, including any specific or extended information will be done as an illegal act regardless of the end form the information ultimately takes. This includes copied versions of the work physical, digital and audio unless express consent of the Publisher is provided beforehand. Any additional rights reserved.

Furthermore, the information that can be found within the pages described forthwith shall be considered both accurate and truthful when it comes to the recounting of facts. Therefore, any utilization, in any form - correct or otherwise, will make the Publisher free of responsibility as to the actions taken outside of their direct purview. Regardless, there are zero scenarios where the original author or the Publisher can be deemed liable in any fashion for any damages or hardships that may result from any of the information discussed in this document.

Furthermore, the contents of this document are solely for informative purposes only and hence should be regarded as universal. As such, the information is given without the guarantee of its validity or interim quality.

Trademarks that are mentioned are done without written consent and can in no way be considered an endorsement from the trademark holder. This document likewise provided trademarks without written consent, and should not be seen as advertisement from the trademark owner.

TABLE OF CONTENTS

Introduction 1

Chapter 1 *Numerology – The Secret World of Numbers* 3

Chapter 2 *What Numbers Can Reveal About You* 10

Chapter 3 *Numerology And Other Metaphysics* 12

Chapter 4 *Your Birth Chart* 16

Chapter 5 *Maturity Number* 25

Chapter 6 *Life Path* 29

Chapter 7 *Expression Number* 35

Chapter 8 *Personality Number* 39

Chapter 9 *Attitude Number* 43

Chapter 10 *Soul Number* 48

Chapter 11 *Hidden Passion Number* 55

Chapter 12 *Money Number* 60

Chapter 13 *Numbers And Your Relationships* 63

Chapter 14 *Balance Number* 80

Chapter 15 *Double-Digit Number* 88

Conclusion 103

Description 104

INTRODUCTION

Congratulations on purchasing *Numerology Easy Guide for Beginners* and thank you for doing so.

Numerology has been used for centuries. It is a metaphysical tool that can provide you with insights about yourself and others, and this book will teach you everything you need to know.

In the first chapter, we will look at what numerology is. We will go into its past and learn how it came to be. We'll also cover the different types of numerology and how you can use it in your own life.

Then the next chapter will cover the things that numerology can reveal. There are a number of things that a numerology chart can tell you about yourself and others, and it can help guide you in your life, which is what we will look at in this chapter.

In chapter three we will look at how numerology relates to other metaphysical tools. These will include astrology and tarot. You'll be surprised to find out that there is a big connection with all of them.

In chapter four we will talk about finding your birth chart. We will talk about each of the numbers that make up the birth chart and what they can tell you.

Starting in chapter five, we will begin to look at specific numbers you can find in numerology. The first is the maturity number. We'll go over its significance, what it means, and how to find yours.

In chapter six we will go over the life path number. This is the most important and popular number in numerology and it is included in your birth chart. Again, we will go over what each number means and what it can tell you about yourself.

In chapter seven we will talk about the motivation number. This can help you to figure out what you need in order to make changes in your life. Once you learn how to find yours, you will also learn what it means.

Then we will talk about your personality number. This number plays an important part in your life and will likely tell you more about you than you know.

Then we will talk about how you can find your destiny number. This will help to give you insights about your future.

Next on the list is your soul number. This is another important number that you will find on your birth chart. We will go over how to find yours and what it means.

Next, we will go into your hidden passion number. This is some fun information for anybody who feels like they are missing something in their life. This number may just give you the information you are looking for.

Then we will talk about your money number. This will show you some important information about your relationship with money. This can be helpful if you are looking to improve your financial situation.

The next chapter will go over how numbers can help you with your relationships. Certain numbers are more compatible with others, and we will go over these combinations. Just know that it isn't the only factor in a good relationship. It shouldn't be used as your only reason to be in a relationship.

Then we will go over the balance number. We'll cover how to find them and what they mean for you.

Lastly, we will cover the importance of double-digit numbers. These are different than the master numbers that we will cover early on in the book, so make sure you pay special attention to these.

This book provides you with the basics of numerology and can help you to get started. There are many other numbers within numerology that you can learn about that tell you different things. These numbers will give you a great starting point, and you will be able to provide people with their own birth chart if you want.

CHAPTER 1
Numerology – The Secret World of Numbers

Numerology is simply the study of numbers that play a role in your life. Numerology can reveal things about the world and people because it is a universal language of numbers.

If you already know a little something about astrology, then you likely already know some things about numerology. There are many similarities between the two, but they both use different methods to find their insights and information.

Numerology views the world as a system that can be broken down. Once broken down, we can see the basic elements of the universe, which are numbers. You can use these numbers to help you understand yourself and the world.

By knowing that the world is dependent on numbers, numerologists are able to take different elements of a person and then turn them into important numbers through different methods. They use the numbers to you better understand yourself and maybe learn some new things about your traits and purpose. They use things like our expression number, life path number, and heart's desire numbers.

Numerology's History

Nobody knows exactly where the practice of numerology originated, much like many ancient philosophies. Babylon and Egypt are where some of the earliest numerology records have been found. There is some evidence that suggests that numerology may have started thousands of years ago in Japan, Greece, China, and Rome.

Out modern numerology is most often credited to the Greek philosopher Pythagoras. While we don't know if he did invent it, he created some theories behind it. His theories took the numbers to a brand new level. These theories are why Pythagoras has been given so much credit in modern numerology.

Pythagoras, along with many other philosophers of that time, believed that since mathematical concepts were easier to classify than physical things, they were more truthful. St. Augustine of Hippo believed, much like Pythagoras, that everything had numerical significance and the mind had to investigate and look for these secrets, or they were revealed through divine grace.

After the First Council of Nicaea in 325 AD, not following the beliefs of the state church was seen as civil violations in the Roman Empire. Christians didn't view numerology favorably, so they were labeled as unapproved beliefs along with other types of divination. Despite this, the spiritual significance that had been assigned to "sacred" numbers didn't go away. The "Jesus number" is still used within the conservative Greek Orthodox practices. While the church resisted numerology, many have argued that numerology is mentioned in the Bible.

For example, number seven and number three hold important meaning in the Bible. The biggest example of this is that the world was created in seven days. Jesus asked God three times if there was any way he could avoid crucifixion. His crucifixion was held at three in the afternoon. Seven days was the normal length of famine and any other God-imposed events. It is also seen as a symbol of change along with the number eight.

There were alchemical theories that were similar to numerology. For example, Jabir ibn Hayyan, a Persian-Arab alchemist, framed his experiments around numerology that was based on substances in the Arabic language.

In Sir Thomas Browne's literary discourse *The Garden of Cyrus*, numerology plays a large role. In his book, he demonstrated that the number five as well as the Quincunx pattern can easily be seen all throughout nature, design, and the arts.

The name numerology was coined by Dr. Julian Stenton. He has also worked to bring awareness and recognition to numerology in modern times. Not much else is fully understood about the creation of numerology, but it has gained much popularity in today's world.

How does it Work?

As you will see, most of the equations for finding your numbers are quite simple, but the way it actually works is complicated. The most complicated part of reading is understanding what the different numbers mean when they are put together in one person. This is what most people go to a numerologist for. They want to know what all of their numbers together mean.

The idea behind numerology is that universe and a person's life is greatly affected by their birth name, birth date, and several other factors surrounding the person. This is why numerology can provide a lot of information. It can provide a person with astounding information about their self or another person.

In numerology and many other metaphysical tools, coincidences do not exist. This means that your birthday and name were meant to be yours and affects your journey and characteristics.

A Numerology Reading

A reading in numerology involves several calculations. The different calculations can go very deep using several different combinations and numbers with different meanings. Even when it is a basic reading that only involves the core numbers, it can tell you quite a bit. However, since numbers are infinite, so is a person's numerology chart. It can continue to be read as an ongoing thing and from several perspectives.

Numerology readings begin with a person sharing their full birth name and birth date. These are the main tools that are used to find the different numbers of your reading.

The most common numerology reading is a natal, or birth, chart. This is similar to the astrological natal chart in that it gives you a guide to your life. It shows your weaknesses, strengths, and who you can become. Different than the astrological natal chart, your numerology birth chart is simpler. This chart consists of six numbers. Three of them are calculated from your birth date and the other three come from your birth name. They are your attitude, path, birth, soul urge, personality, and power numbers.

While all of these numbers are important and can provide special meanings, the most important one is your life path number. This is the most important number because it tells you the path that you have to take in order to feel fulfilled in life. It lets you know who you truly are at your core, and who can become if you live up to your full potential, much like your sun sign in astrology.

Numerology Methods

There are several different systems that give letters a numerical value. Some examples are the Hebrew numerals, Greek numerals, Armenian numerals, and Abjad numerals. Within Jewish practices, gematria is the practice of assigning meanings to words based on the numerical value.

- Latin Alphabet

Several numerology systems use the Latin alphabet to assign letters a number value. Some of the various interpretations include Pythagorean, Chaldean, and Hebraic.

- Pythagorean System

This comes from Pythagorean Numerology. Pythagoras started out his theory of numbers by finding the numerical relationships of numbers and musical notes. He discovered that he could explain the vibrations created by stringed instruments through mathematics. His method of numerology uses a person's name and birth date. The name number shows what the person's outer nature is. This includes how they present themselves to those around them. It requires the person to provide you with their name as it is written on the birth certificate. This means if there was a typo at that time; it has to be used because it has a spiritual significance. Each letter in the name is assigned a number ranging from one to nine.

- Chaldean System

The Chaldeans were the rulers of Babylonia from 625 to 539 BCE. This is why this system is sometimes referred to as the Babylonian numerology system. They used their numerology system to find the energy changes that happen when a person thinks or speaks. When somebody speaks, the voice comes out at different frequencies that affect them and the people around them. The Chaldean system doesn't use the number nine because it is believed to be a sacred number because it is connected to infinity.

Seven Facts

Now that you have a good understanding of numerology and what the numbers mean in your life, let's take a look at some interesting facts about numerology that can help you.

1. Negative and Positive Numbers

Every number in any numerology reading comes with negative and positive features that you have to pay attention to. While numbers should be balanced in negative and positive aspects of their whole self, it's important to understand how those numbers are influenced. These factors include your outlook and the other numbers that correlate with the various aspects of your love, health, business, and career.

2. Master Numbers

The master numbers in numerology are 11, 22, or 33. These numbers have deeper meanings. The meanings of them could be good or bad, but that depends on the context. This is why it is important to properly interpret the master numbers. They should be used as guidance for certain circumstances that can impact your life that need to be addressed.

In most readings, double-digit numbers are split apart and adding together until you reach a single-digit number. But, if a calculation reaches a master number, you stop. You don't have to reduce it any further because they have their own meaning.

The master number 11 often relates to faith and instinct. It can also show anxiety and fear, so make sure you read into it carefully.

The master number 22 is known as the master builder. This is a good indicator of success and ambition, though it normally needs guidance or other perspectives.

The master number 33 has several meanings within different readings.

It's important to remember that you can still combine these master numbers to get the single-digit numbers, two, four, and six. This will provide you with a more well-rounded reading.

3. A Guide to Life

Numerology is more than insight into who you are. There are a lot of advocates of numerology who have attributed the success to numerology. Numerology provides you your barriers. It can also help to guide you based on what your position is within the universe, possibly adding to your success. Powerful and deep feelings that most will find hard to understand become more apparent. It can help inspire you to switch your life up completely.

4. Believing in Numerology

There are many numerologists who have said that once a person starts to look more into their numerology chart, they are so amazed by what it reveals about their core issues and desires that they will continue working towards enlightenment and discovery. Once you have really found the accuracy in these readings, you can start to find your own truth. Plus, you can learn what your inner feelings have been trying to tell you.

5. Weakness and Strengths for Purpose

Most people, because of how accurate numerology readings are, will encourage other people in their life to try using numerology as a way to figure out their weaknesses and strengths. With this discovery, you can provide yourself with a good idea of the things you should and should not do in your life. Plus, you will be able to move forward with purpose.

6. A Lot of Numbers and Meanings

While there are a lot of online tools and calculators that will give you your numbers, it's important to know that there are quite a bit of number and meanings behind the different combinations. It takes some research and knowledge to really understand what all of this means for you. You might be able to type your birthday into an online calculator and receive your life path number; it can't show you what this number really means for you personally.

7. From Birth

The most fascinating thing about numerology is that all of the readings are based on the time that you became part of the universe in your current human form. From birth. No matter whether or not you like your birth name, or when your birthday is, all of it is important. Be proud of your birth date and the name you were given at birth. In numerology, there is a reason for everything.

CHAPTER 2
What Numbers Can Reveal About You

If you want to discover insights into your life path and character, numerology is one of the easiest tools. The day starts and begins with numbers. Every second of our lives revolves around numbers that have the ability to change our lives. The meanings of numbers are so deeply ingrained in them that just the smallest amount of focus can change our lives.

When you find the numbers on your birth chart in a later chapter, you will find six numbers that work together to describe you as a person. The life path number exists alongside your expression and personality numbers. The latter share your outward appearance and inner goals.

Many people will find that they have extremes in their numbers. For example, a person with a life path number 8 and personality and expression number of 2 have dueling natures. This means they will have to find a way to bring balance between these two.

From all of the numbers associated with numerology, there are four that play the biggest part of your life. These are your life path number, expression number, motivation number, and the birthday number.

The life path number is a combination of your birth date. This number tells you your identity at birth and what your basic characteristics will be throughout your life. When you look at this number, it can provide you with insight into what direction you need to take in order to get the most from your life.

The expression number is found from the values of your birth name. This number can reveal information about your expression of life and how it will affect the life path you have to follow.

The motivation number, or soul urge number, comes from the value of vowels in your name. This number can help you to gain insight as to what motivates you. This relates most with what you want to be and what you want to accomplish.

The birthday number tells you what direction your life will take.

When you read your numerology chart, you have to take several other factors into consideration. Certain factors can influence the energies of your main numbers. These factors don't have the same impact as your core numbers, they should still be taken into account when you are doing your reading, otherwise, it can come out inaccurate.

There are some numerology readings that involve forecasting numbers that tell you about important milestones. These can tell you the ages where you will have big things happening for you. The hardest thing you may find is digesting the information in a logical way.

Master Numbers

We've touched on this a bit, but let's look further into master numbers. Master numbers are 11, 22, and 33. When you reach one of these numbers, you do not have to continue to reduce them down to a single digit. There are some numerologists that will use all repeating numbers as master numbers, but most don't.

Master numbers indicate almost complete development of the traits associated. Responsibility and freedom are burdens that come along with having master numbers in your essential numbers. You have the ability and freedom to decide whether or not you will let them be dominant, but when you do this, you have to act responsibly. You could also ignore the power of this number, but this will keep you from reaching your strengths. It can hinder your true mission.

If you can harness the power of these numbers, it can make a life-changing turn for you. However, these tend to be the people who experience the most challenges.

The important thing is to learn how to understand and use your numbers as a whole. They don't work individually.

CHAPTER 3
Numerology And Other Metaphysics

Numerology has close ties with astrology and tarot. These three metaphysical tools have various similarities, and just as many differences, but they can help aid your understanding of the other. Before we look at the connection between them, let's take a quick look at what tarot and astrology are.

Astrology

For centuries, cultures have looked towards the sky for guidance. This has led to the practice of astrology. Astrology is simply the study of the relationships and patterns of the planets and stars. This is used to help a person find meaning in their life.

The premise of astrology is that the movements of the planets influence different moments in time. Since we are all parts of the Universe, our moment of birth becomes part of the celestial clock and plays a role in our life. The planets are always moving, engaging with our fixed birth date.

If life starts to seem like it is a series of meaningless events, astrology is able to help you understand that maybe things are happening for a reason. It can help to show you your natural strengths and inner contradictions. The astrological birth chart can help you to understand yourself that will never stop showing your new things.

When astrology and numerology are combined, you get astro-numerology. The most common methods of astro-numerology have been created on the Indian subcontinent, but likely had origins based in Greek, Egyptian, and Babylonian methods created in Alexandria during the Hellenistic Era. We will look at a few because these methods can become advanced and require an in-depth understanding of astrology and numerology. They also require time and place of birth to create the astrological chart before you can apply the other techniques.

One of the most fascinating methods of astro-numerology is where numbers are used to represent the planetary forces. This is most commonly used by astrologers and arithmancers in the West and East with a slight difference between the two.

- The number one is associated with the Sun.

- The number two is associated with the Moon.

- The number three is associated with Jupiter.

- The number four is associated with Earth. There are some discrepancies on the number four and its associated planet. There are some who call the planet the "negative Sun." Indian astrologers associate it with Rahu. There are some who associate it with Uranus.

- The number five is associated with Mercury.

- The number six is associated with Venus.

- The number seven is associated with Neptune, but there are some astrologers who associate it with the "negative moon."

- The number eight is associated with Saturn.

- The number nine is associated with Mars.

- The master numbers are associated with Pluto and Uranus.

When the negative sun is mentioned, it refers to the negative characteristics of the Sun, which includes stubbornness and egotism. The negative moon refers to things like superstition, fantasies, and instability. However, the positive parts of seven are a lot like the positive aspects of Neptune.

As you can see, some people have combined astrology and numerology to create a whole new system. When Einstein shared his mathematical theories and explained the order of the Universe, he talked about numerology and astrology, as well as the vibrations that numbers give out. These numbers are the basis of the universe and help to explain how the psyche works.

This means that astrology and numerology rely a lot on mathematics. The birth charts for each cannot be created or understood if a person doesn't understand the meaning of the numbers. While there may not be a need to have a complete understanding of astrology in order to do numerology, some basic understanding of planetary influences can improve the reading. The reason for this is that the numbers are ruled by the planets, sun, and moon, as listed above. They are also related to the astrological zodiac sign. To match up the zodiac signs, you follow the planet that rules the zodiac.

This means that numerology and astrology can easily be used together. They are a great way to map out your horoscope and can help you find meaning in life.

Tarot

Tarot involves a deck of 78 cards. Each has its own story and imagery. They are broken into two sections, the major arcana, and minor arcana. The major arcana are 22 cards that represent the spiritual and karmic lessons in life. The minor arcana are 50 cards that show the trials and tribulations that people experience every day.

The minor arcana cards have 16 court cards that represent the 16 personality characteristics that people may express. They also include 40 numbered cards that are organized into four suits. Ten cards of each represent different situations that you might encounter every day.

Tarot works as a storybook for life. It mirrors the soul and helps improve our inner wisdom. When tarot is consulted, it will show the exact lesson that you need to learn in order to live an inspired life.

Each card in the tarot deck is assigned a specific number. The meanings behind the numbers one through nine have the same meaning and symbolism in tarot. If you are using numerology with tarot, you may have to add up some of the numbers. For example, the hanged man is number 12. You would reduce this number to three in order to reach a stronger understanding. Again, the sun is

19, so you could reduce it to one. But the experienced person would like to look at the individual digits as well.

It's easy to find the numerological associations with the minor arcana. Aces are associated with the number, and the rest of the cards in each suit are numbered two through ten. Ten would then be reduced to be one as well. In readings, the numbers show subthemes and patterns which have to be considered along with the cards.

This means, if you wanted to, you could find the tarot card that is associated with your life path number, or any other numerology number.

CHAPTER 4
Your Birth Chart

Numerology, like astrology, provides people with a birth chart. In this chapter, we will go over how to find your birth chart using your birth date and name.

A birth chart is made up of six numbers. Three of the numbers come from your name and the other three come from your birth date. This will describe the kind of person you are, the way you express yourself, the career path you might want to follow, your likes, your dislikes, and other insights that can help you understand you.

There are many other numbers within numerology, some of which we will go over in this book, but for the sake of the birth chart, we are only going to go over the six most commonly used.

Numerology also has master numbers. These are the only double-digit numbers that are using in readings, 11, 22, and 33. If you reach one of these three numbers in any of your calculations, you do not have to reduce them down to a single digit. It is best, though, to understand the meaning of the single digit numbers before going into these master numbers.

There are many of these six numbers that have their own chapter later in the book. If we don't go over the exact meaning of each of the numbers, just know, it will be covered later on. This is just to help you discover the numbers on your birth chart.

Birth Date

- Life Path – (MM/DD/YYYY)

To reach your life path number, you add up all of the numbers in your complete birth date. You continue adding them together until you reach a single digit or a master number.

The life path number shows you want your general ups and downs will be in life. Basically, it is the flow of your life.

For example, if your birthday is 12/19/1960, you would add the numbers in a month, day, and year together to get 3, 10, 16. You continue to add each down to a single digit to get 3, 1, 7. Then you would add these together to get, 3+1+7 = 11. You would stop at 11 because it is a master number. Their life path is an 11.

Here's another example, the birthday 8/15/1992. Again, you'd add the month, day, and year together individually to get 8, 6, 21. Then work it down to 8, 6, 3. 8+6+3 = 17, and that would become an 8.

- Gift Number (DD)

The next birth chart number is the gift number. This uses the day that you were born. The gift number tells you what your talents and gifts are. It tells you what talents come easiest for you.

The gift number lets you know what skills or talents you have that can help you to reach your life's purpose. Please remember, that there is not a single number that controls the course of your life. A lot of components make up each number. Tools like numerology are only meant to help you understand yourself better, but you have to use the information as a whole and as guidance. You shouldn't simply pick and choose the areas that serve you.

Taken from the example above, if you have the birth date 8/15/1992, you would add 1+5 to get 6. Their gift number would be 6.

You also have the choice of leaving your birth date unchanged, so for this person, they could have the gift number 15 as well as 6. This can provide more insight into who you are.

Since we won't be covering gift numbers later on in the book, here are the meanings of the gift numbers.

1. If you are one, then you are a born leader. You are great at starting things. You love to work with other people because they motivate you. People will naturally follow you.

2. If you are a two, then you are gifted at compliments. You like taking on a background role, but you are willing to support anything that you view as a worthy cause. You are sensitive and intuitive.

3. If you are three, then you are social and silly. You help people feel better and motivated. You often have encouraging words for anybody going through tough times.

4. If you are a four, then you love receiving information and putting things together. You have a knack for discernment. You are great at finding the truth and sharing what you found.

5. If you are a five, then you have a strong mind and you love to travel. You are great at letting people know that they should have fun and find their purpose. You don't like to stick to one place mentally or physically for too long.

6. If you are a six, then you are a natural caretaker. You are great at making people feel comfortable and you like to take care of other people's wants and needs. You can also spot beauty.

7. If you are seven, then you are intuitive and psychic with a lot of questions. You think out-of-the-box and you view things differently than most. You need a lot of alone time.

8. If you are an eight, you are great at exercising power. Business and money are important to you. You are great at leading people when you are balanced.

9. If you are a nine, then you are a humanitarian, motivator, and diplomat. You are great at inspiring other people by being their example. When you have mastered something, you are willing to help others.

10. You lead by example and are in touch with the Spirit. You know that there are other forces guiding you. You do things based on your gut and inspired action. View 1.

11. You passionately lead. You are great at inspiring other people when you have become emotionally involved. You are unstoppable when you believe in what you are doing. View 2.

12. You are great at communicating thoughts and ideas. You have the ability to make those things into reality, and you can spot the areas you can expand on. View 3.

13. You seek out ideas and information. You love to learn new things through various means. The ways you share and teach are unique to most. View 4.

14. You are a wanderer with a wide variety of tastes in things, places, and people. You attract different situations. You love being diverse and cultured. View 5.

15. You are artistic and intelligent in many different ways. You want harmony in life and you are willing to go to great lengths to bring about change. You love helping others. View 6.

16. You love finding hidden meanings. You are able to spot the deeper meanings in poetry, music, art, film, and movies. You like to talk about deeper things with people you are close to. View 7.

17. You are a great leader who can go it alone. You are great at inspiring others to do things without having to say to tell them what to do. People follow you when you are at your most balanced. View 8.

18. You are great at bringing things to life and giving back. You are mature beyond your years and this gives you the appearance of somebody who can help people. You love helping others find their power. View 9.

19. You have experienced a lot in life and this makes you well rounded. You have the gift of starting and finishing things that you believe are important. View 10 and 1.

20. You are an empath and can pick up on the energy of others. You have the ability to pick up on subtle information. You have to make sure not to be too emotional. View 2.

21. You have the ability to express yourself in many different ways. You have a lot of intuitiveness when it comes to ideas and thoughts. View 3.

22. You are a natural creator of things and ideas. You are great and putting things together. It could be that the information is used to connect the dots or to make something random seem relevant. View 4.

23. You work to express yourself in a spiritual way. You are a free spirit when it comes to connecting with others on a deep level. You often come off as erratic, but you follow your heart. View 5.

24. You love to be around beautiful people and things. You understand harmony. You are great at making ugly things more attractive. View 6.

25. You are great at being alone and with others. You love being with yourself, but you also attract others that bring balance and fun to your life. Conversations and travels are important. View 7.

26. You have drive and power to get the things you want, but you remain humble and are concerned enough to help people you care about. You attract others that you can easily help. View 8.

27. You have had a lot of experience that has helped you grow emotionally and spiritually. You often help others who are less fortunate. You like to share and learn about "taboo" topics. View 9.

28. You are a natural leader and have the ability to get whatever you want. You don't see a problem with establishing a powerful network. You have a strong business mind. View 10 and 1.

29. You are a humanitarian that has a message. You know how important it is to give to people who are less fortunate. The most important thing to you is providing spiritual encouragement. View 11 and 2.

30. You often talk about the things that others think and do but aren't willing to say. When you open up, you are able to share things that can help people to view things in a different light. View 3.

31. You are great at attracting information and people that help you to grow as a person. You know a lot of information. You love to learn and you love to share your information. View 4.

- Attitude Number (MM/DD)

The next number on your birth chart is the attitude number. For this number, you add up the month and day of your birth and continue to add until you reach a single digit.

This attitude number represents your attitude and outward persona. This is how other people see you. This represents your outward appearance or the first impression that people get from you. This number can provide you with a good "success ratio." It helps you to figure out how you can tap into and use your innate abilities.

Sticking with the birthday of 8/15/1992, you would figure out the attitude number by doing, 8+1+5 = 14, 1+4 = 5. This means their attitude number is 5.

That is the last birth chart number that is found using your birth date. Let's move into the three numbers found using your name.

Name

The last three numbers of your birth chart are found by using your full name as it is written on your birth certificate. You have to use the name you were given at birth to get an accurate reading you can't use a nickname or anything that you have changed it to over the years. You also need to use your birth name and not your married name. Your full birth name is what influences who you are. The three numbers are your personality number, soul urge number, and your expression number.

Every letter of the alphabet is assigned a number. There are two different systems for changing letters to numbers, that is the Chaldean and Pythagorean systems. The only difference between the two is the Chaldean doesn't assign the number nine. For this, we will be using the Chaldean chart.

- Chaldean Numerology:
  - 1
    - A, I, J, Q, Y
  - 2
    - B, K, R
  - 3
    - C, G, L, S
  - 4
    - D, M, T
  - 5
    - E, H N, X
  - 6
    - U, V, W
  - 7
    - O, Z
  - 8
    - F, P

We are going to use the name Damito Jo Ann Hurst for out examples below.

- Expression Number (Full Birth Name)

The expression number tells you how you tend to express yourself. It is how you feel the most comfortable sharing your message.

To get your expression number, take your full name as it is written on your birth certificate and assign each letter a number based on the chart above. You then add up the digits in each name until you reach a master number or single digit, and then add them together.

For our example it would look like this:

{D(4) A(1) M(4) I(1) T(4) O(7)} {J(1) O(7)} {A(1) N(5) N(5)} {H(5) U(6) R(2) S(3) T(4)}

Damito = 21 = 3, Jo = 8, Ann = 11, Hurst = 20 = 2

3+8+11+2 = 24 = 6

- Soul Urge Number (Vowels)

The soul number shows you what your innermost desires are. These are the things that your soul is attracted to. This is also known as your heart's desire number.

To find your soul urge number, you add up the vowels in your full birth name. If we use the same name from above and use only the numbers associated with the vowels we would have, 1+1+7+7+1+6 = 23. This would give her the soul urge number of 5. We will cover the meaning of the numbers in the soul number chapter.

Please note, if you have a Y in your name since a Y can be a vowel or a consonant, the Y is considered a vowel if it doesn't come at the beginning of the name or it sounds like a vowel.

- Personality Number (Consonants)

The personality number tells you what your outward personality is. It tells you the amount of yourself that you are most comfortable revealing to other people.

To find out what your personality number is, add up the numbers associated with the consonants in your full birth name, and then reduce them down to a single digit.

For our example, we have, 4+4+4+1+5+5+5+2+3+4 = 37 = 10 = 1

Our example has personality number 1. We have a chapter dedicated to personality numbers where we will go over their meanings.

Now that you have your birth chart figure out, let's dive deeper into the meanings of the numbers.

CHAPTER 5
Maturity Number

The first number we are going to go over is the maturity number. Everybody has one. The energy and vibrations of this really kick when you hit your 40s. This is one of the only numbers that doesn't have a precise calculation. The influence of your number will incrementally increase between the ages of 35 to 50.

The maturity number is basically your destination. At some point in your life, you are going to reach that point. This will typically come as your midlife message. This is typically the point where people have their midlife "crisis" or they experience settling down.

There are several ways in which the maturity number shows the true self. It guides the second half of life after you have gone through the "been there, done that" years. The majority of numerologists will agree that this number hits your full force by age 50 and will continue to follow you and influence the rest of your life.

The gift of this particular number that you will "suddenly" be hit with this feeling that you don't have the patience or time to waste on stuff that isn't pushing you toward your ultimate goal, whatever your goal is. Let's take a look at how to calculate your maturity number.

To calculate your maturity number, add together your expression number and life path number.

If a person's life path number was 8 and their expression number was 6, you would get 8+6 = 14. We would add 1+4 to get 5.

The interesting thing you may find about your maturity number is that it isn't always in harmony with the rest of your numerology profile. This means that you could experience ease or friction when it comes to experiencing the conflicting energies or if the maturity number provides an overabundance of energy.

Keep in mind, the maturity number shows the true you.

Let's go into what the maturity numbers mean.

Ones are moving toward reevaluating the meaning of being independent. You feel like you need to take some initiative, to become a leader, and to take some risks toward your own achievements in anything that you feel passionately about. When it comes to ones, there tends to be a shift in experiencing issues related to independence coming center stage. There will come a time when a situation highlights your independence or dependence, your ability to make a connection with others, and if you act in a controlling and domineering way.

Twos are reevaluating what using emotional sensitivity to help yourself or others means. You want to use your diplomacy, to work within groups, and become open to relationships. There is often a shift that will cause sensitivity issues to become center stage. You will experience situations where you experience a strong sense of self in relationships. This means that you don't need outside approval to feel good.

Threes will reevaluate what creativity, joy, and expressiveness mean. You feel compelled to step into your creativity, express artful and joyful communication, and enjoy socializing. This shift will bring creativity to the center stage. You will experience situations where you feel an increase in enthusiasm and joy, social interaction, and communication.

Fours will reevaluate what it means to have limitations. You feel compelled to work more towards your practical goals, create processes that help you reach them, and to leave a lasting impression. You will often experience issues when it comes to restriction and limitation. You will have situations where you will adopt step-by-step processes to help you get where you need to be, and you will learn the difference between micromanaging and managing.

Fives will reevaluate what it means to reach freedom. You feel compelled to work with freedom, living your life full of adventure and travel, and embracing uncertainty, flexibility, and progressive change. You will reach a shift in life around issues of the disciplined use of freedom. You will experience moments of tactile and vivacious living, change and versatility, and excessive behaviors.

Sixes will reevaluate the meaning of being in service to and loving your family. You feel compelled to work toward your duty and service to help others, affection, and compassion. You will reach a shift related to modulating responsibility. You will experience situations that highlight meddling or self-righteous behaviors, the strength of intimate relationships, and being compassionate to others.

Sevens will reevaluate the meaning of spiritual contemplation and introspection. You want to learn more about yourself through specialization and solitude, philosophical thought, and intuition. You will often feel a shift related to truth-seeking. You will have situations where you need alone time, time for writing or research, and time for spiritual fulfillment.

Eights will reevaluate rewards through their accomplishments. You feel compelled to work with your talents with managing and organization, to reach success, and to use your authority in a wise way. You will notice a shift when it comes to achievements within the material world. You will experience more moments as the lead, to accept financial abundance, and to work to help humanity.

Nines will reevaluate what providing selfless service to humanity means. You will feel pulled to helping others without thinking of personal gain, letting go of your "self," and not attach a certain outcome. You will feel a shift related to balancing your needs with other people's needs. You will have experiences where you will be of a higher purpose, to reach your spiritual path, and use your talents in a philanthropic way.

We also have the master numbers, so:

Elevens will start reevaluating the same things as twos reevaluate. Elevens will also fight with your ego, being pulled toward leadership and fame, and becoming an "introverted extrovert." You will experience a shift when it comes to creativity, sensitivity, and overcoming obstacles. Your challenges will reside in the intensity your experience live, in how you will be put to the test, and emotional and physical sensitivity.

Twenty-twos will reevaluate the same things as fours reevaluate. They will also have to deal with being opinionated, blunt, and rigid in their approach. They tend to be a "know-it-all." You will find intensity in how you experience life, choosing security over the whole picture, and choose defeat over endurance.

Thirty-threes will reevaluate the same things as sixes reevaluate. They will also have to find with being a "bossy pants," and feeling pulled towards leadership and fame. You will feel a shift when it comes to responsibility, co-dependence, and emotional sensitivity. You will struggle with perfectionism, carrying the world on your shoulders, and relationship challenges. The is the rarest maturity number.

CHAPTER 6
Life Path

The life path number is simply the sum of your birth date. The numbers show who you were from the moment you were born and the traits that you will always have. The life path is the most important number we will discuss in this book. It is the nature of your life's journey.

The majority of numerologists believe that everybody has past lives. Before being born into this current life, you would have taken the time to look over your previous life while figuring out what you want to learn this time. This means that your birth date is a combination of numbers that you picked. These create your blueprint or your "soul's contract." Within this contract is all of the lessons that you have agreed to learn this go around on earth.

This number offers you unchangeable information. You can't change when you were born, whereas your name can change because of conscious decision or marriage.

We quickly went over how to find your life path number in a previous chapter. Now, there are some people and sites that tell you to add the numbers straight across. With our example from above 8/15/1992, they would do 8+1+5+1+9+9+2. Yes, this will still get you to the number 8, but there are some instances where it could bring you to the wrong number. For the life path number, you must begin by adding the individual numbers together until you get three single digits, then you can add them together. Sometimes if you add straight across, you will get a master number where there isn't one. Let me show you.

Take the birthday 6/3/1968. If you add the numbers straight across, 6+3+1+9+6+8, you would reach the master number 33. Now, let's see what we get when worked the correct way:

6, 3, 1+9+6+8 = 6, 3, 24 = 6, 3, 2+4 = 6, 3, 6

6+3+6 = 15 = 1+5 = 6

They should have the life path number of 6 and not 33. I know most people are thinking, but its addition. No matter how you add the numbers together, it is supposed to give you the same number, but, as you can see, there are exceptions. If you don't believe me, let's look at another example.

Let's look at Lenny Kravitz's birthday: 5/26/1964

If added across you get, 5+2+6+1+9+6+4 = 33

5, 2+6, 1+9+6+4 = 5, 8, 20 = 5, 8, 2

5+8+2 = 15 = 1+5 = 6

His life path number should be 6 and not 33.

Now that we have our life path numbers, let's take a look at what they all mean.

Life Path 1 means that you live a life of leadership. You are charged by your individualistic desires, a need for independence, and personal attainment. There are a lot of political leaders, corporate leaders, and military generals who are a one. When you have the positive traits of a one you have a mind that will allow you to accomplish a lot, full or creative inspiration, and holds a lot of enthusiasm. You are great at getting things started. You do your best work with challenges and obstacles head your way. You have nothing but determination and the ability to lead others. You have a natural flair of taking charge.

There are a lot of ways where your negative side can appear. The one is great at leading, but they lack as a follower. Unfortunately, there are times when you have to follow before you can lead, and this can be a hard time for the one. When this life path isn't completely developed and showing the negative side, the person can come off as extremely dependent, especially in the early years. You are likely very dissatisfied with where you are if you are displaying the negative traits.

Life Path 2 means you are a fair and balanced individual. Twos are able to see both sides of any situation or argument, and this is why people will often seek you out as a mediator. When you are placed in this role, you do a great job at settling disputes with an unbiased flair. You have a sincere concern for other people. You see the best in others and want the best for them. Twos are open and honest and excel in all types of group activities. You aren't the type to dominate a situation or group. You are great at compromising, and as a team member, you don't demand recognition or praise.

If you display negative qualities of a two, nervous energy will be a big part of your life. This may make you come off as an extremist. Nervous tension can turn your easygoing attitude into outrage, which will seem off-key for you. You can sometimes be over sensitive. Sometimes your strength is your greatest weakness. Twos tend to be plagued by indecisiveness. The biggest obstacle is likely passivity and state of lethargy and apathy.

Life Path 3 means you are a people person. Threes are open, social, conversationalists, friendly, and warm. You are a great talker, in that you are fun to listen to, but you are just as great of a listener. You welcome other people into your life and you know how to make them comfortable. You have a positive approach to life. You are openhearted and sunny. You need a constant supply of similar people. Threes are the romantics. The giving nature of three will often attract demanding partners.

Threes who are living within the negative side of this life path become so delighted in the joy of living that they end up becoming superficial and frivolous. They like don't have much sense of purpose. Negative threes can end up becoming an enigma, and for no apparent reason can become moody and retreat. It is not uncommon for threes to become escapists, and find it hard to settle down. Try to guard yourself against becoming intolerant, impatient, overly optimistic, or critical of others.

Life Path 4 means you are great at carrying out orders and persevering. Many fours are happy and content taking orders and doing the work, but many will end up as a manager or entrepreneur. No matter which role they find themselves in, they demand just as much from their self as they do others, and sometimes more.

Fours are great planners and organizers because of their ability to see things in a practical way. This is partly due to their perfectionist side. It is important for them to plan things. Fours function best when under the gun and facing problems.

Life Path 5 means you are a compassionate and freedom-loving person. You tend to want to extend your freedom to all of humanity and you are concerned about others, their welfare, and their freedom. Abraham Lincoln was five. You hate boring work and routines. You don't do well sticking with everyday work that has to be finished. Fives tend to be the happy-go-lucky type. They live for today and don't worry about tomorrow. You need to find a career that will provide you with thought-provoking work instead of redundancy.

Fives don't like to be tied down. They aren't promiscuous, but it is important that their partners understand their nature. They don't want to feel like they are being controlled. It's important to have a lot of people in your life who aren't all that serious and demanding.

Life Path 6 means you are a natural nurturer. You natural parental instincts exceed everybody else by far. In the office and at home, you are the head and the caretaker. As a six, you may have a lot of responsibility within the community, but your life revolves around the immediate home. Conservative convictions and principles run deeply in your character. This life path is leadership by example. You accept responsibility and pick up the burden when needed.

Understanding, balance, and wisdom are your cornerstones. You function with compassion and strength. There are a lot of burdens associated with this number. On rare occasions, responsibility is passed on to somebody else. If you reject responsibility, you will likely feel uneasy or guilty

Life Path 7 means you have an affectionate and peaceful soul. You guard your personal connections carefully. You are great at detecting deception and insincerity. You don't have a lot of friends, but once you make a true friend, they are there for life. You have to really get to know a person before you let the walls down. You are probably refined and charming with a quick wit and poise. People will often see your reserve as aloofness, but it's not. It's simply your cover up for your insecurity. You are not a joiner.

You are a deep thinker and can learn things from anything. You rely on experience and intuition instead of advice from others. The seven has a lot of highs and lows. It may be hard to find stability in emotions.

Life Path 8 means you are here to govern, organize, direct, and lead. You are goal-oriented and ambitious. You want to use your abilities and ambition to carve out a satisfying niche. A positive eight has a lot of potential for creating far-reaching ideas and schemes. You also possess the independence and tenacity to follow through. You were born to become an executive.

This is the most common life path to become workaholics. You are great at spotting good people and bringing them into your endeavors is a trait that shouldn't be overlooked. You have an inspirational streak that makes for a great leader. This path is concerned about status and success. You want to be recognized for what you do. You are likely very well suited for politics or the business world.

A negative eight can become dictatorial and will suppress the enthusiasm of others. Rewards and material possessions become the most important thing to them, even to the point that they neglect their own peace of mind, family, and home. Eights need to avoid discounting other people's opinion.

Life Path 9 means you are honorable and trustworthy. They also don't harbor any type or prejudice. This is a tall order, but you are the type of person that feels deeply for the less fortunate, and if you can help, you will. The nines of the world hold an elevated position when it comes to responding to mankind.

You are commanding and can make friends easily as they are attracted to your personality. A nine's deep understanding of life is often manifested in the literary and artistic fields. You are probably able to express your emotions through music, writing, painting, and other forms of art.

It's not uncommon for a nine to become negative and fight the challenges and realities of their purpose because being selfless isn't easy. You may find it hard to believe that lacking personal ambition and giving back can give you satisfaction.

Life Path 11 is a master number and is the most intuitive. It connects you to your subconscious, to a knowing and gut feeling. 11s also has all of the qualities of a two. The negative qualities of 11, stressed energy, shyness, and anxiety, are balanced by two's inspiration and charisma. 11s need to be focused on a concrete goal. Don't deny your instincts.

Life Path 22 is the "master builder." These people can spin their wildest dreams into reality. They have the intuition of an 11 and all of the traits of a four. They are disciplined and ambitious. Not all 22s are practical. This can be a problem for 11s and 22s. They are capable of greatness but shy away from things when there is too much pressure.

Life Path 33 is known as the "master teacher." With the combination of 11 and 22, dreams and intuition go through the roof. There is a lot of potential for this number. They are focused on humanitarian issues and have no personal agenda. They can throw themselves into a project that goes past practicality. They are highly knowledgeable, but they fact-check before they share their ideas. This is a very rare number. It is only significant if it shows up as one of your core numbers in the birth chart.

CHAPTER 7
Expression Number

The expression number is found using all of the numbers in the name you were given at birth. It reveals your shortcomings, abilities, and talents that you will experience during your life.

Why does the expression number use your name? Your name shows what your personal history was up to the time you were born. Whatever your history, it has molded you into you who you are. Your parents, before you came to life, picked up on your vibrations and picked your name accordingly. Your birth name is what you were meant to receive.

In order to figure out your expression number, we have to change the letters to numbers. In the birth chart chapter, we used the Chaldean chart, which doesn't use the number 9. For this example, we will use the Pythagoras chart so that you can decide which you would prefer. Here's the Pythagoras chart:

- 1
  - A, J, S
- 2
  - B, K, T
- 3
  - C, L, U
- 4
  - D, M, V
- 5
  - E, N, W

- 6
  - F, O, X
- 7
  - G, P, Y
- 8
  - H, Q, Z
- 9
  - I, R

We will do the same as above and write out your full birth name and it is associated numbers. We'll stick with the name Damito Jo Ann Hurst just to see how different the number ends up being since we are using a different chart.

D(4) A(1) M(4) I(9) T(2) O(6) = 26 = 8

J(1) O(6) = 7

A(1) N(5) N(5) = 11

H(8) U(3) R(9) S(1) T(2) = 23 = 5

8+7+11+5 = 31 = 4

As you can see, her expression number went from 6 to 4 depending on the charts. The Pythagoras chart seems to be used more often, but whatever feels right to you is the one you should use.

Here are what each expression number means:

Ones are courageous, leaders, ambitious, and independent. You are great at influencing others. Since ones are warriors, front-runners, and pioneers, some of the most fulfilling jobs could be inventors, religious leaders, self-made millionaires, businessmen, and politicians.

Twos are open-minded and friendly, with a strong intuition and are great at working with others. You do best when working alongside others rather than as the leader. It can sometimes get frustrating because you don't always get the recognition you deserve. It's essential that you have harmonious and close relationships.

Threes are expressive, inspiring, optimistic, and outgoing. You have a certain bounce about you that inspires others without much effort. You are very social, yet you need to learn how to accept other people in your life. You have a lot of potential within the arts. You are self-expressive and creative, but make sure you don't scatter your talents.

Fours are the foundation of enterprises. You are very structured and methodical. Jobs like lawyers, managers, government officials, bookkeepers, and accountants will make you the happiest. You also tend to be attracted to music and arts, but you will also bring along your love of order.

Fives are the free spirit, excitement, and adventurer of the world. Freedom is what your life revolves around, and you have to make sure you bring this forward with your talents. You want to do everything at least once. You tend to be scattered and unorganized, yet you are great in communication and could end up being happy as a lawyer, politician, or salesman.

Sixes are caring and loving, and often put others before themselves. You are trustworthy and find honesty to be extremely important. You are creative, but your talents often go undeveloped because you sacrifice your time to help others. You would make a good gardener, artist, psychologist, or teacher.

Sevens are driven by knowledge and truth. You have a gifted analytical mind and you crave answers. You like philosophy, scientific matters, and mysticism. You will likely be drawn to being a philosopher, banker, technician, investigator, or researcher.

Eights are great at achieving greatness. You are competitive and strive to be the most successful in your field. If you find discipline, money and authority come to you. You are an amazing leader and a good judge of character. You can become intolerant and stubborn if your focus too much on your success and result.

Nines are humanitarians and idealists. You want to change the world. You are happiest when involved in things that benefit the public good. Healing, teaching, environmental protection, law, and politics may be good for you.

Elevens are powerful but are not yet aware of this power. You are sensitive and have always felt you were different. You have to learn how to control your energy; otherwise, you will experience tension and emotional turmoil.

Twenty-Twos are dreamers and want to make a mark on civilization. You have no limits to what you can do or what you can dream up. Your ability to help mankind is larger than normal. However, this number presents risks that you may not want to take. This can create frustration because you know you are made for greater things.

Thirty-Threes are teachers who are driven by enlightenment and spiritual wisdom. You are a lot like the six but on a grander scale. You can be physically damaging to others, but when you are positive, you can bring comfort and healing.

CHAPTER 8
Personality Number

It's hard to be objective about yourself. Even the people closest to us have a hard time telling you how they view you. The personality number is the one number that can provide with this type of insight.

This number is your hallway leading to the true you. It is the aspects that you are comfortable with showing others from the start of the relationship. With some time, you will allow others to see the deeper parts of your nature. Eventually, you will show who you truly are. In other words, you will show them the other numbers in your birth chart.

This number will often work a lot like a censoring device, both when it comes to what you show and what you allow others to show you. It is what influences the types of information and people that you allow into your mind and heart.

This is why your personality is more protective and narrow in its meaning than what you truly are, and is typically the part of you that you find the hardest to recognize. It helps to screen out the things that you don't really want to deal with, but it also attracts the things that relate to your inner self.

Either for good or bad, this is the first impression that people get from you. It will either welcome them or scare them off.

To calculate your personality number, you will add up the consonants in your name. We will use the Pythagoras chart for this reading as we did in the last chapter. You should already have the numbers associated with your name.

We will stick with the name that we have been using. Remember, if at any time you reach a master number, stop adding those numbers together.

For the first name, we will have the letters:

D(4) M(4) T(2) = 10 = 1

For the next two names:

J(1) = 1

N(5) N(5) = 10 = 1

For the last name:

H(8) R(9) S(1) T(2) = 20 = 2

Then we would add them all together:

1+1+1+2 = 5

This person would have a personality number of five.

Let's take a look at the meaning of each number:

Ones radiate an efficient and dynamic energy. You come off as capable and in control. You like seeing effort and courage when faced with difficulties. Others can tell you aren't willing to be pushed around. You care about your appearance. You are seen as a pioneer. You are creative, original, and a risk taker. You should make sure that you don't come off as unreceptive or aggressive. You can come off as intimidating if you don't soften your outward appearance a bit.

Twos come off as unpretentious and friendly. You are warm and soft. Others view you as gentle. You attract people because you appear unthreatening and warm. You are clean and neat and you prefer comfortable clothing. You have a sex appeal that people are attracted to. You are a great listener, understanding, and patient. Others feel loved and important around you. You likely faced a lot of negative criticism growing up, which made you shy. While you may not be shy anymore, you still have some vulnerability. People often underestimate your strength.

Threes are full of life. You come off as charming, and uplifting. People love to be around you because you are fun. You are the life of the party. Threes are often very beautiful. You are optimistic and extroverted. You like the finer things in life. You are a romantic and you love to give affection. You will have to work at developing lasting relationships. You may rely too much on humorous and superficial conversations.

Fours are a family person. You strive for the security, consistency, and intimacy of family. You are a protector and provider, but the family may take this for granted. You play a big role in your community. Your consistency in your plans will usually pay off in a secure and comfortable future. You are consistent and reliable. People trust your judgment. You dress in a practical way. You present yourself as correct and in control. You respect the dollar. You worry about the security of you and your family's future.

Fives are stimulating. You brighten up any social situation with your original and fresh ideas. Your conversations are full of wit and you have a quick tongue. You love freedom and adventure. You are optimistic and upbeat. You infect others with your optimism. You tend to indulge in alcohol and food. You love anything stimulating, and this often includes drugs, alcohol, food, and sex. Discipline is important. You are sometimes irresponsible when it comes to satisfying your urges. People expect the unexpected from you, and if they don't happen, they are surprised by it.

Sixes are full of compassion and understanding. People feel your fairness and warmth. You will often attract people in need of comfort. People will often unload their burdens on you. You want to keep harmony and will often sacrifice your own desires to help others. You are domestic and hospitable. You are a great parent and love children. Your financial views aren't that logical.

Sevens are different and mysterious. Others view you as studious and serious. You are self-sufficient. You notice wisdom quickly, and others respect you. You don't typically show compassion or warmth, even though you likely have both. You tend to be withdrawn and it takes a lot to get to know you. You come off as dignified. You are not one for talking unless you are talking about something you are passionate about.

Eights are powerful and strong. You are very impressive and you are able to influence, possibly even intimidate, others with your force. You are naturally authoritative. You attract people through your enthusiasm and competence. You are confident. People will often ask your opinion because of your effectiveness and sureness. While eights tend to have a strong constitution, they are often prone to reckless eating and drinking habits, heart disease, ulcers, and indigestion. You can sometimes come off as egocentric.

Nines are aristocratic and impressive. You always come off as noble. You are in complete control of the image you display. You are charismatic and elegant. People admire you. You will either pull others in or repel them completely. Some may try to belittle you because they are jealous. You should make sure you stay down to earth and work with others. You also have compassion for humanity. You are sympathetic and compassionate.

Elevens have worked to gain confidence and to work through their natural shyness. Throughout childhood and into your 20s, nervous energy could have caused nail biting tendencies or you express this nervousness in some other way. You are intuitive and sensitive. You have to be careful with who your friends are. You come off as a safe harbor to others. You are great at listening and are understanding and patient. Arguments drain you.

Twenty-Twos are consistent and reliable. You come off as the cornerstone of businesses and people rely on you for the work you do. You long to create something that will have a lasting impact. You have a lot of power, whether you know it or not. This power caused you to feel uncomfortable and awkward during your early years. You inspire enthusiasm. You are a family person. Your image is contradictory. At one time you will come off as unique and with a lot of potential. Then there are times where you come off as inferior or insecure. This has created self-doubt and low confidence. But it creates a lot of energy when you combine this with the heightened characteristics of 22.

Thirty-Threes inspire confidence. You want to keep peace and you will sacrifice your own needs to do so. You are viewed as a parental figure. You are protective, faithful, and romantic. You tend to be vulnerable to criticism and praise. At your core, you are a six. This gives you the chance to be influential within your community. You appear to be more concerned about your personality than your appearance.

CHAPTER 9
Attitude Number

Has anybody ever told you that you need to "lose the attitude?" Maybe people tell you that you are a very positive person and have a good attitude. This all related to your attitude number in numerology. This is sometimes referred to as the achievement number. This number shares a couple of things:

- This number typically tells you what your first impression or outward appearance is to the outside world.

- There are some numerologists who think that this number can provide you with a good indication as to what your "success ratio" is. It lets you know how you can successfully tap into your gifts and use them to reach satisfaction, prosperity, and abundance.

For this number, you will use your birthday and your birth month. You do not have to use the year.

If your birth date is 8/15/1992, you would do this:

8, 1+5 = 8, 6 = 8+6 = 14 = 5

This person would have an attitude number of five. Let's take a look at what each of the numbers tells us.

Ones will often appear to be an innovator with a tendency to act independently and put their own unique spin on things. You typically avoid asking for help, even in times when you could use it. You are achievement driven, competitive, and self-motivated. You do your best work when you are in a leadership position. You struggle with self-esteem problems, so you will likely seek out praise for your work to keep you going. You will likely come off as driven and competitive, but you may seem a bit stand-offish.

Ones will often struggle with acting out rebelliously or become depressed when you are not allowed to be creative, independent, and original.

Twos will often be seen as a person who gets things done through collaboration, accommodation, diplomacy, and kindness. You tend to be easygoing and tend to show nervous tension because you are more concerned with taking care of everybody else's emotions. You are love-centered and naturally intuitive, so relationships are the most important thing for you. You are extremely compassionate and are rarely bored since you will be busy helping others, and you love to connect with others through your heart.

You will likely struggle with taking things too personally and can end up being overly emotionally sensitive.

Threes have the greatest potential to move u in the world when they are able to be socially active, creative, and dynamic. You will often give off the impression that you are the creative genius, entertainer, and the joker. You are social, smart, witty, and funny. You also have a tendency to be scattered and hard on yourself. You are naturally a joyful person and your happiness tends to be contagious. If you end up becoming depressed, everybody around you will feel it as well. Friends are extremely important to you and you are great at uplifting and inspiring others.

You may struggle with burying your dreams because you are afraid of being criticized or because you allow your emotional baggage to take control.

Fours with often appear to be at their best when they get to use the management and organizational skills. You appear to be a reliable, loyal, honest, and determined person. You always have an up-to-date calendar and lists. You like to get things done. You are a naturally gifted teacher and have several other types of expertise. This could range from mechanic work or construction to being a farmer and raising chickens to whatever else that you find interesting. Your emotions tend to come off as elusive. You will often seem to be somewhat detached from the world. You often tend to be the Devil's Advocate when you have to face dishonesty or an infraction of something that you feel very strongly about.

You may struggle with inflexibility limiting your success. Stability and security play a big role in your life, yet you tend to cut yourself short from reaching that success when you don't let yourself move outside of your box.

Fives tend to do your best work when you move with change and progressiveness when you are fearless and adventurous. You succeed the most when you are able to act in a "larger than life" kind of way. You are fun, playful, and tend to enjoy being the center of attention. If you are struggling to live up to your crazy standards, you may end up becoming a martyr, or you may stir the pot wherever you are. You are full of life, flirty, and gregarious. You are up for change and freedom tends to be the most important thing in your life.

You tend to struggle with swinging from one extreme to the next. You are either too myopic and fearful or you are too scattered and free-wheeling. You often attract restrictive circumstances so that you can define your meaning of freedom.

Sixes work the best when they are being service-oriented, diligent, and conscientious. You tend to give off the impression that family, beauty, and home are your main focus. You are probably a self-proclaimed perfectionist. You tend to focus on helping other people instead of yourself. You are a control freak, but you are also great at managing emergencies and damage control, whether professional or personal. You are a natural nurturer and you tend to work well with children, animals, and the elderly. You don't like being bossed around, so you will naturally want to work alone. You are a connoisseur of beauty, magnetic, and a visionary.

You tend to struggle with controlling your sense of responsibility, both with others and yourself. Your tendencies to be a perfectionist will often dampen your ability to be accepting and happy to others and yourself.

Sevens often appear their best when they can tap into their innate skills of being an intuitive genius, strategic thinking, and data analysis. You live very differently than most people in the world. You will often come off as mysterious and aloof to others. You will likely analyze things, ask a lot of questions, and study things. You are an amazing observer even when other people think you aren't paying attention to anything. You are a strong intuitive type, so you are great when you can merge your intuition with your scientific thought-process. You have a lot of wisdom that you can use to help the world.

You will likely struggle with your sarcasm and sharp tongue, and you might skim the surface of life with being superficial.

Eights often come off as being more powerful than others, confident, and strong-willed. You tend to be controlling, opinionated, and blunt. You despise lolly-gaggers or people who want to waste time. Time is money, and both of these things are extremely important. You place a lot of importance on money because of everything it can do for you. It can provide you with respect, power, freedom, security, and stability. These are all things that you strive for. Eights aren't a light little jaunt. There will be challenges along the way when it comes to self-empowerment and money. You strive for respect and you leave lasting value. You are also extremely resilient. You have to think of abundance, positive, and big dreams and then chase after them

You tend to struggle with authority figures. You often struggle with releasing the past, with getting beaten down by struggles, and with challenging and difficult experiences that happened early in your life.

Nines will often appear to be natural teachers, intuitive, and gifted. You are a compassionate leader. You are happiest when you can serve your humanitarian purposes, whatever those may be. You have a lot of charisma and people tend to be pulled towards you and believe that you are the one in charge. You are amazing when it comes to faking it 'til you make it. You have to learn to give and receive. You also need to learn how to enjoy the rewards of your endeavors. You work with your heart, you will be at your best. You are a naturally creative person and are great in the arts. You have to learn how to let go and live in the moment.

You will likely struggle with being emotionally drained if you don't create boundaries with others because you care so deeply about everybody's struggles. You will often lean toward fanaticism and you struggle with active listening.

Elevens will often appear like twos, but with more intensity. You kick everything up a notch and you do your best work when you get to be the inspired healer in whatever fashion you so choose. You are over-the-top emotionally sensitive, extremely intuitive, and creative. You may appear to be anxious, dreamy, and flaky.

You will likely struggle with the intensity and challenges of a master number. As a master number, you have to remember that you are running a marathon. You have to pace yourself.

Twenty-Twos you come off as an extremely intense number four. You have the most powerful number, but it's a challenge to master the energy connected to it. You are here to leave a lasting impression that can help people every day. You are practical. You may come off as rigid, literal-minded, and self-absorbed.

You may struggle with the master numbers challenges and intensity. Like the 11, you have to pace yourself.

CHAPTER 10
Soul Number

This number has been called the heart's desire number. This number can peel back some layers of your numerology chart. Your life path number can give meaning to the direction of your life's journey. Your destiny number shows your unique offerings to the world, talents, and gifts. Your soul number unlocks the spiritual, eternal, deeper you; the you that is usually hidden from the world.

Knowing this personal code can reveal your fears, passions, urges, inner cravings, and everything that motivates you on a spiritual, deep level. Your soul number reveals the force behind what your soul was sent here to do in your lifetime.

When you have uncovered your number, life will begin to make sense. Anxiety and depression usually lift as your soul's stirrings can finally be given the fuel it needs to thrive, nurtured, recognized, and find meaning within the world.

You will only use the vowels in your full birth name. You have already figured out your life path number so all you have to do is go back and just add up the vowels. You are going to do this for each name. You will add the vowels in your first name, middle, and last name individually and then add them together. If one of your names adds to a master number, the master number doesn't get reduced. It just gets added to the other name numbers and then reduced down to a single digit number.

What about the letter "Y?"

The letter "y" is hard to figure out since it could be used as either a vowel or consonant. It depends on the way it is being used within each word and the sound it makes.

Use these rules to work out whether you need to add it into your calculation:

Use it as a vowel when:

- It is the only vowel sound in the syllable like Kylie, Terry, or Gryffin
- Y is in front of a vowel in a different syllable and gives another vowel sound like in Hyacinth or Nya

Use it as a consonant when:

- Y is used in the place of a consonant that has a hard sound like Toyota, Yuliana, or Yoda
- If Y is after a vowel in the same syllable and doesn't give another vowel sound like in Nataliya, Maya, or Grayson

Let's take a look at the meanings.

Soul Urge One: If you have a soul number of one, your soul's urge wants to be your driving force in life. You believe that what you do, say, and feel has a lot of value in the world.

You want to be heard and you want others to follow you. Your trust your instincts usually above the perspectives and views of others. You have the makings to be a pioneer and great leader.

You have had many problems with authority during your lifetime but not because of you self-assuredness which means others look up to you for direction and guidance no matter what position you take.

You are loyal and committed but your dominance means that others are silent in your presence. You might not notice that you have hurt other people's feelings that you have left behind. You have to be careful that your confidence doesn't get confused with arrogance. Make sure your desire for progress won't cause unneeded competition.

Even though you won't be fulfilled if you aren't in a position of power or authority, try to make friends on your way up the ladder. You don't know when you might need loyalty in the future.

Soul Urge Two: If you have a soul number of two, you want to be loved, admired, and needed by everyone. You need to connect with others and get motivated by relationships. You are tactful and sensitive and are always trying to keep balance and harmony. Everyone cooperates easily when you are around. Life begins to feel uncomfortable fast at the first sign of drama or conflict so try your best to keep the peace since it is what you are good at.

You might have problems with trusting yourself during your life. It isn't because you don't value yourself, you just need somebody else's opinion to connect, contract, or measure up to yours. If you don't have an external reference point, you might feel lonely and lost.

You have a strong connection to others that means you are a team player and a valuable contributor to the entire process. You have to make sure your sensitivity and kindness don't leave you vulnerable or too open. Making strong emotional boundaries will make sure you aren't taken advantage of.

Soul Urge Three: If you have a soul number of three, you have the desire to express and cultivate your personal magic. You are original, witty, and inspiring and you can instinctively see the good side to each situation. You seek fun and pleasure and this makes you a magnet for other people. You share your shiny perspective with all who are around you.

You are a performer and love an audience that adores you. You can achieve great recognition and fame in life, especially in the arts. You might be a tad scattered and disorganized in the way you approach life. You make you look a bit disloyal or uncommitted, it is vital for you to learn how to devote and channel your creativity to larger, fewer project while growing.

You are always going to have critics in your life, this is all just part of the territory. Your challenge will be to develop fierce self-love and to rise above them.

Soul Urge Four: If you have a soul number of four, you want to find stability, order, and beauty in this chaotic world. You find satisfaction in doing the simple, practical, domestic, or repetitive chores since you feel more in line with your essence when you can restore harmony to situations that are unbalanced. You create systems and love making plans and organizing the world around you. Other people feel secure and stable when around you and you are asked for advice often.

You might fear uncertainty or change and this means you might miss out on chances to grow. It is important that you have the space for spontaneity and do this often that will take you out of your comfort zone.

You are very generous, patient, and loyal. Your attitude could be received as a bit too unkind or harsh but never intentional. Developing better tact and empathy would serve you well.

Soul Urge Five: If you have a soul number five, you want to experience as much variety as you possibly can. You have a thirst for adventure and an inquisitive mind that can only be satisfied if you are on a quest. Your passion is travel and you feel alive when you are out on the open road experiencing new things and meeting new people. This might cause you to become restless or jaded and struggle with commitment. If you feel like you are being hemmed in, you will find a way to rebel quickly.

You inspire others with your enthusiasm and you make friends easily. Keeping these friendships is hard because when the excitement wears away you don't like opening up to people.

You trust that the Universe is going to look after you but don't share this trust with others. Learning how to be vulnerable to others is a challenge but one that might bring you a lot of fulfillment and strength.

Soul Urge Six: If you have a soul number six, you like caring and nurturing others. You have a gift for making the conditions right so other people can reach their highest potential and flourish. You love everyone. You need to provide for others and a sense of what they need.

You are happy when you see all the positive results and see the people around you happy and thriving. This selfless approach to life can lead to you neglecting yourself and your needs. You have to make sure your energy doesn't get depleted and you care for yourself regularly just like you do for others.

You have some perfectionist tendencies which lead to having high expectations of yourself and others. This means it can be hard for you or anyone to reach the goals you have set. This will lead to resentment and disappointment, so you have to let go or complete happiness and fulfillment will never be reached.

Soul Urge Seven: If you have a soul number of seven, you want to understand what the world around you means. You are a seeker of knowledge and will always be on a quest to find the "whys" and "hows" in life. It might be mystical, literary, historical, or scientific but you have a yearning to want to know more.

Since you have a questioning nature, you will feel like you don't belong in this world. You can't understand why other people can accept things at face value. You will instinctively separate yourself away from them and might be looked at as an outsider.

You are unique and your perspectives are very valuable. Finding healthy outlets and expressions for your theories and thoughts are vital if you want to fulfill your potential and gain the trust of your peers.

You have to work to develop self-trust because no matter how much research and groundwork you do, your truth will be found inside.

Soul Urge Eight: If you have a soul number eight, you want to find prosperity, status, and power. You get motivated by achievement and success especially if it is financially rewarded. This isn't a yearning that is selfish; your desire to control comes from the need to improve other people's lives and will distribute wealth accordingly. You know the industry, trade, and commerce and you want to benefit the ones you love.

You are ambitious and confident and have a lot of stamina. Your sense of purpose might come across as domineering but you just want to have the success that you have worked hard for.

The challenge for you isn't to be overcome by material gains, but to go that extra mile and use your power and money for the greater good. You are a leader so make sure you lead by example and have integrity all the time. You can instill great respect and trust to others, so it is vital that you don't abuse the power you have been given.

Soul Urge Nine: If you have a soul number of nine, you desire to make the world a better place. You have the heart of a humanitarian and want to leave a legacy of love and wellness everywhere you go. You are deeply altruistic and you want the best for everyone. You have a rare gift of seeing their souls and knowing what they need.

You are positive and that can't be waived. You have the perspective of a visionary. You have the ability to believe and see the best outcome of any situation. You want to impart your insight, experience, and wisdom to other people but you have to be careful that you don't come across as overbearing. You are sometimes regarded as a person who has the answers could mean that other people might rebel or resent your advice. They might resist thinking for themselves if they are around you. You have to be careful that your desires won't interfere with other people's needs to find their way. They need to make their own mistakes.

It is important to learn the art of fair exchange. You have a generous spirit and you can easily give without needing to receive anything in return. You want to believe you are setting a good example but you might be creating unhealthy imbalances of energy.

Soul Urge Eleven: If you have a soul number of 11, you need to trust your inner voice and to express this to the world confidently. You are insightful and sensitive soul and it is likely that you have the ability to channel high-frequency information. You might have other psychic gifts, too. This is a challenge as you might feel nervous, too empathically aware, or ungrounded in what other people feel.

You have a calming influence on others. You are creative. People might be drawn to you because they sense your high frequencies by just being near you. You may feel as if you are on a search for spiritual truths and try to see these in other people. Your challenge is to go inside yourself and find the peace that you desire.

Soul Urge Twenty-Two: If your soul number is 22, you want to catalyze the world's transformation. You are an architect and a visionary of the future. Your perspectives inspire others and give people the goals they need to constantly evolve. You are practical, stable, and grounded so it isn't likely that you think that your vision is anything but ordinary.

Just like number four, others will feel stable and secure when you are around them. You inspire confidence in them. You make a great organizer, manager, and leader of people. You will start to realize your true calling when you finally see your greatest vision materializing with other people's help.

You have to make sure that you are following your calling. Don't get lethargic and confined within your comfort zone. You are destined for great things but self-belief and courage have to come first unless your talents get frittered away.

CHAPTER 11
Hidden Passion Number

The hidden passion number is one that gets repeated in your name. It shows a certain field of expertise or a specific talent. When talking metaphorically, this talent has the power to shape your life. It gives you the desire to create and express a particular ability.

When you have talent this number demands that you use it. You have to experience that part of you. You have to live according to its nature. By doing this, the hidden passion can shape your personality and will guide your life.

Even though it isn't considered as one to the core number in your reading, it is one of the more powerful numbers on your chart. A numerologist will pay special attention to this particular number.

In order to find your hidden passion number, the first thing you need to do is write out your complete birth name. This means your first, middle and last name as written on your birth certificate. Each letter will get a number according to where it is located in the alphabet. You can use the chart back in chapter seven. When you have given each letter a number, write down how many times a number shows up.

Your hidden passion number will be a single digit number that shows up most frequently. You can have more than one hidden passion number if more than one number ties for the most frequent. You will have multiple hidden passion numbers.

Let's look at the name: Darla Faye Hurst. You first need to assign each letter a number: D-6, A-1, R-9, L-3, A-1, F-6, A-1, Y-7, H-8, U-3, R-9, S-1, T2. As you can see there are four letters with the value of one. This means that Darla has a hidden passion number of one.

Here are what the different numbers mean.

Ones want to always stand out. You have a desire and ambition to accomplish things. You are very competitive and what to be the first and best in all the things you do. You are very creative and energetic. You can influence and dominate other people. You have extremely developed political skills and could submit to manipulation unless you have extremely high ideals.

There might be times when you won't have any confidence, especially when you are very young. Don't fear you are strong enough to overcome this problem. You are a leader, a warrior, and a survivor. There are politicians and athletes that have this number. Having six or more numbers in your name can make you tyrannical, violent, aggressive, and bullish.

Twos tend to be very intuitive, sensitive, and considerate. You try to find pleasant and peaceful environments. You try very hard to create harmony with your coworkers and peers. You work great in group environments and you usually serve as a peacemaker. You may look like you are timid and shy and even though you like being around people, you have an inner fear. You don't like roughness and noise.

You constantly look for information. You commit to your job and perform your duties with a lot of persistence, patience, and competency. You are usually one pillar in any organization. People will naturally rely on you.

You tend to worry a lot about insignificant details and might waste time on unimportant affairs. You are too sensitive and can be hurt easily. Your feelings will get in the way of your judgment. You have a great ear for rhythm and music and you love the arts. You love having beautiful things around you. You have delicate and fine tastes.

Threes are often the party animal. You are very social and are great for expressing yourself around your peers. You love to go to parties as much as you love to entertain. You are very popular and a great friend. You are very talented in the arts like painting, music, acting, or writing. You have to be around excitement. If things get dull, you will begin fantasizing and might begin to exaggerate.

You can motivate and inspire people around you. You have been blessed with a large amount of charisma and charm. You are overly optimistic and this makes you a rolling stone. You always think the grass will be greener on the other side.

You have to have focus and discipline to make the best of your talents. You have a tendency to be a bit scatter-brained. You have to be careful not to indulge or become selfish in too many things that gratify your senses.

Fours are the rock. You are very organized and systematic. There aren't many goals that you can't reach. You have self-discipline, perseverance, and determination. You have a tendency to be realistic and practical. People look at you like a rock because you are very reliable and loyal. You worry about the welfare of the people in your community. People have faith in you and the way you care for them.

It is important to you that you love your job because you need steadiness and security of daily schedules. You absolutely don't like the unexpected. You have an incredible eye for details. You love being in nature and the beauty it gives you. You love the organization that comes with natural law. You have great understanding and judgment when estimating how valuable a plan is or how feasible an enterprise might be. Your concentration is excellent. Your home and family life are extremely important. Your love for them runs deep. You are very protective and loyal.

If you have more than four – fours in your name you have to watch out so you won't get obsessed with details. You could become boring, narrow-minded, or rigid.

Fives are the adventurers. You love new challenges, change, and travel. You are versatile and adaptable. You are good with words and have a talent for languages. Public relations, promotion, and writing suits you best.

You are a tad impulsive and sensual. You love satisfying your senses and this could get you in trouble. Overindulging in drugs, sex, drink, or food can be common in people who have six or more fives in their name.

You have a quick tongue, a great sense of humor, are original, and resourceful. You have a very strong desire for freedom and it will take a lot of discipline and effort to keep doing what you have started. You have a tendency to give up on situations or projects too early. You get interested in a lot of things and this can make it hard to apply yourself to just one area. You get interested in too many things.

You are unconventional. You are happiest when you are committed to your job and relationship. You tend to wander from job to job or partner to partner and this makes have strong relationships or a successful job very difficult.

Sixes want to serve their community and the people they love. You are capable of being a teacher, counselor, or healer. You are very responsible and are willing to sacrifice a lot. You have to be careful that you don't become a doormat for people who don't appreciate you or want to take advantage of you.

You have strong opinions and are idealistic. You can get a bit self-righteous even though you are generous and a humanitarian. You are a great partner and parent. You will always be willing to listen to other people's problems but you have to be careful and not interfere. You will always help your fellow human beings.

Sevens have a wonderful intuition and a very developed mind. You work well with ideas that are abstract because you are very intelligent. You like being alone to study, meditate, and contemplate. You are drawn to metaphysics and philosophical studies. Even though you can be cynical and skeptical of things that you can't easily prove. You have unusual insight and understanding. You are a deep thinker. You don't like wasting time on petty or trivial matters.

You are a perfectionist and a specialist. You have a unique ability to come up with different solutions to problems and you can be extremely convincing if the subject is of interest to you.

You could become depressed, melancholic, and self-centered. Being lonely is common with people who have a lot of sevens in their name. They have to figure out how to be alone without feeling lonely. The balance of nature and faith is a necessity. You might seem that you are hard to get to know, alien or different but when people finally "get to know" you, they will respect and love you.

Even if you have a tendency to keep to yourself, you are generous when you love and are truly concerned with other people's happiness. You just don't demonstrate that love.

Eight's actions are motivated by material rewards and success. You are goal-oriented and believe in effort. You can impress and dominate others with your common business sense and vision. You are a born organizer and manager, the people that work under you like you. Authority and leadership are obvious, but it isn't wise to be dominant, demanding, and forceful.

You have a great judge of character with an ability to sense people's weaknesses and strengths. You might be tempted to abuse this since eights like to be ruthless and greedy.

The ability to sense where people are coming from will be better served by your natural instincts. Even though most eights have an advantage in the world of business and can help you find success can make your life hard. There are many frustrations and tests that you have to overcome. What is more important is having the right perspective and balance regarding matter and spirit needs to be attained. You have to have a family that you are proud of. You need status in order to feel rewarded. You might like to show your success and wealth.

Nines are compassionate, generous, and warm. You would be happy and do well in anything that gives you a decent living but helps everyone. The number nine is responsible for most of the creative geniuses. This means you are probably very artistic. Those talents are usually suppressed and sometimes won't come to surface until midlife or later in life. You want universal knowledge and insight.

You're emotional but your feelings aren't always sensible and could be suppressed. You might get caught up in ideals and dreams without staying practical. You have enough enthusiasm and fire to attract support from others. You are very independent and are driven to do your own thing. The ability to speak well have saved many situations.

CHAPTER 12
Money Number

As we have established, numbers can have qualities other than showing quantity. They have rich meanings and can relate to all areas of our lives and this includes money. If you would like to know how you can make the most money in life and how well you will do financially, numerology will tell you how you will deal with the money in your life.

You can find your money number by taking the day you were born and adding a one to it. If the result is a double-digit number, keep reducing until you have a one digit number. Here's an example: Johnny Depp's birthday is June 9, 1963. The only number you need to worry about finding the money number is the day he was born on the 9th. So we will take the number nine and add one to it: 9+1=10. Reduce the 10 down 1+0=1. So he has a money number of 1. There are a few exceptions to the rule. If you get a master number of 11 or 22, you don't need to reduce down any further.

Let's take a look at what the different numbers mean.

Ones always have a monetary advantage in their lives. It also represents beginnings and you might find yourself beginning new things. It doesn't normally get into debt since the money will stay with the person who made it. You are a leader and are great at building wealth. The prosperity that is attracted to you gets enjoyed by your employees. You like to have complete control of your money. You don't mind doing hard work if you are paid well for it. You might make the decision to work for yourself and be your own boss so you can control all the money. You are a leader and can build wealth easily.

Two is the worst number to have financially. It doesn't reflect wealthy because it implies that what is made is shared with others. This number symbolized disappointment and delays along with putting the concerns of others above your own. Number two is generous to a fault. You love luxury and this can send you spiraling into debt. You do have strong intuitions when you need to make decisions about your money; both when making it and when spending it. You will be able to tell if a proposal is bad or good even if the deals say differently. It may take you some time to learn to trust your instincts.

Threes have the ability to talk your way into money. You have strong communication skills that you can use to make a living. You make a great salesperson, life coach, or entertainer. You don't have any problems creating money-making ideas. You might find that following through on these ideas is rather difficult. This is a lucky number but one characteristic of this number is the money gets spent as quickly as it is made. This makes it hard to accumulate funds. You might find yourself always being "a penny short and a day late" even if you are wealthy. You will get into debt easily but can get out of it just as easily.

Fours are usually attracted to career choices that are conservative. You will work your way up the ladder into a position of responsibility and trust. You expect to work hard and long for what you get and will take pride in every step along the way. This number isn't destined to be poor but you will work hard for all the money you make. If you don't have good discipline, you can stay in poverty. This number has been voted the least likely to ever win the lottery. It does have the ability to grow a lot of money from investments.

Fives are usually drawn to careers that involve making deals, selling, and buying. You love a variety I work and will change careers many times during your life. You like being the boss and hate being told what to do. You would love to have a job where you get to travel a lot. You are great at business and thrive if you can stay organized and remain in your budget. You have a philanthropy streak and will treat your employees well. You think that money needs to be given away. The universe rewards you with what you need in life as a karmic thank you for having a great attitude.

Sixes need a stable job to be happy. Job security is extremely important. You can't bear the thought of being unemployed or not having a steady income. The actual job isn't what's important because your family will always come first. You will receive money from family in your life. This number symbolizes abundance. You will inherit some sort of money since this number is all about family and gifts. You will flourish at anything you try and usually won't have to worry about cash. There aren't any extreme financial lows or highs.

Sevens dream job would be working in some sort of technical job that is related to research or science. You love to study and solve problems. You won't have great wealth from your job because you place satisfaction before financial gain. You might face financial challenges because you have an eccentric vibe. You earn quite a lot of money but don't care about it. You are likely to make millions from a wild idea. The bad news is that you could use your wealth for unethical reasons or begin to hoard your money.

Eights are fairly good at making money. You will either hold a high position in a company or be self-employed. You always focus on making money and you like it too much. You have to be sure to create some interests in life so work won't consume you. This number symbolizes big bucks but it can symbolize huge losses, too. This number means that "you need to spend money in order to make money". Many times this number is plagued with expenses to keep up your expensive lifestyle.

Nines love humanitarian organizations and causes. You desire to help others and this can cause you to be way too generous when you give your money and time. You look at money as just a means to an end. It only has value for what you can do for people. This number will attract money effortlessly and easily. You will be prosperous but have a hard time holding onto your wealth for very long. Many number nines will have a natural "Midas Touch."

Elevens will be able to market their ideas to make money. You will need a partner who will push you and make you do your best. You will do well in the creative fields such as editing, composition, or writing. You can do well in humanitarian areas like social services and education. You don't like working in finance or business.

Twenty-Twos will be able to make all the money you want as long as you are working in a field that you believe in. You will do your best work if you believe in what you are doing and it will benefit humanity. You won't work for selfish means for a long time.

CHAPTER 13
Numbers And Your Relationships

Using numerology in love and relationships is a great tool to help improve your romantic life.

Even though it is great to be in a relationship with somebody who understands you totally, you don't want to date anyone who is exactly like you. The Universe would like to keep you on your toes. You are usually attracted to people who are your polar opposite.

This will leave you scratching your head, or banging it against a brick wall, but realize it is for your own good. You will be drawn to people who have the qualities that can balance you. They might have some traits that you would like to learn. If you like to daydream, you might feel safe being around other people who are practical and grounded. If you are sensitive emotionally, you could be drawn to a person who allows things to roll off them. If you connect with a person who has qualities that are opposite of yours, it causes spicy chemistry and this makes both of you become better individuals.

It's a Wonderful Tool

Numerology can help you understand your partner's romantic urges, drives, and desires. This is your owner's manual. Think about it is as knowing what breed of dog you have just adopted.

Your number will show you what you and your partner need to be happy together. It helps you communicate with one another. If you would like to know your partner's love language, the number that will reveal their needs will be their life path number.

This is the most important number to look at when seeking relationships is the life path number. You have to take into account all the numbers in your numerology chart; this isn't the only number you should consider.

Understanding Your Perfect Partner

Note that the information mentioned is just the tip of the iceberg. This information reflects what every number will bring to the forefront, the aspects of each number show the knowledge that we want to acquire and be a master of. IT is quite possible that we will encounter hardships with the very thing we set out to do or accomplish. You have to remember this.

You can use the following to understand and know yourself better and help you pick a partner who has the values and characteristics that are important to you.

1. The Leader

If you have the number one for your life path number, you are a leader. Your purpose is to develop your confidence and creativity in everything you do. You want to learn how you can make yourself different from others, create your independence, and then get on the path that will lead to your goals.

- You are all about achieving, initiating, creative, innovative, and competitive.
- You could be great entrepreneurs
- You are meant to be a leader
- You use "fall forward" to reach your goals
- You are a very creative thinker

Challenges:

- Wrestle with addiction
- Don't have self-confidence
- Can be cynical, judgmental, and critical
- Can't get a sense of your creative gifts, individuality, and independence

Probable Compatibility Profiles

If you are involved with or have a life path number of one:

You need a cheerleader. You need to be praised and positive reinforcements. You need a lot of time to think and process in general but more for dealing with relationship matters. You are creative but need to be encouraged to follow your unique vision. Because confidence will always be an issue for you, you need to have a relationship with somebody who is in tune with your need to be praised and supported. Realize that you have been enrolled in the "School of Hard Knocks." You will experience a lot of obstacles within your lifetime and these are meant to strengthen your uniqueness and not to destroy or bring you down. You aren't living a particular linear existence.

Red Flags:

These people usually have tempers. They are usually in their own head and usually find mutually dependent relations. They are natural leaders so they have to have followers. They will always be active, intelligent, and charming. On the bad side, they could be narcissistic and could acquire that feeling of responsibility with the situation, the persons involved who give judgment and criticism, the possibility of issues relating to addictions and negation. This goes back to a lack of self-confidence.

2. The Mediator

If you have the number two as your life path number, you are a mediator. You create your balance, diplomacy, harmony, and love in anything you undertake. You thrive when you are meeting the needs of a group of people. You are a person who will move and make sure that things happen. You are about love – whether it is receiving or giving. You look for love and possess a giving and open heart. You love partnerships.

- You want everybody to get along, balance, and harmony

- You are very supportive, loyal, dedicated, intuitive, and emotionally sensitive.

- You love to be useful and works better in a group

Challenges:

- Could be aggressive, self-centered, and childish

- Want to please everybody and knows what they want

- Will over give and withdraw feeling resentful

Probable Compatibility Profiles

If you are a number two or involved with a number two:

You are somebody that everyone can count on. You are able to love and want to be in a loving relationship. You are super sensitive, so be careful that you don't get your feelings hurt. You will be in tune with other people's emotions and usually feel emotionally drained. You have to have a large area to completely express yourself or they will shut down. You are a giver and you want to please everyone. You try to avoid conflicts and are a great mediator but you see this as an oxymoron. You are very family oriented.

Red Flags:

You can be a worrier and codependent. You can be a micromanager and champion if you were to allow it. You have a tendency to smother people close to you. If you are working on the destructive parts of your life's mission, you tend to be assertive, aggressive, and antagonistic. You can over give and then withdraw. You will hang on to old matters with resentment. The main things to your personal evolution are acting, setting, and defining healthy emotional boundaries.

3. The Communicator

If your life path number is three, you are the communicator. Your main purpose is to create your sense of emotional sensitivity and self-expression in everything you do. You thrive in the spotlight by performing, entertaining, or any creative way to communicate by writing or speaking.

- Your emotions are the center of your life
- You are joyful and are in your element with communicating, hosting, and socializing.
- You feel your best when you are uplifting and inspiring others.

Challenges

- Hard time following through on tasks
- Debilitating over-thinking and self-doubt
- Emotional lows and highs

Probable Compatibility Profiles

If you are involved or are a life path number three, you are very passionate. You are full of emotional expression and humor. You can be a lot of fun to be around. You are caring and joyful. You have to be heard in the relationship, so you have to be a good listener and care about your inner emotional life. You could develop emotional crushes that never mean anything. Just know that it is your mind's fantasy and not a threat to an actual relationship. You can be a bit of a drama queen. You can handle yourself in a crisis very well.

Red Flags:

You could be married to your projects instead of a person. You could have a battle with depression. If you aren't aligned with constructive elements, you could be prone to procrastination, self-absorbed, and scattered. Sometimes you might hide from your emotions and get cut off from you're an aspect of yourself. If this is the case, you will be very analytical. You could easily succumb to what is called "analysis paralysis" and get overwhelmed when making decisions or following through.

4. The Teacher

If your life path number is four, you are a teacher. Your main purpose is to develop a sense of hard work, stability, security, and process in everything you do. This number is the "slow and steady wins the race" who will thrive if they know the rules, have a sense of routine and security with their lives and are allowed to use their skills.

- You are an excellent organizer and a master of systems
- You are a knowledge sponge and love to share what you know with others
- You work hard and enjoys a job well done

Challenges:

- Struggles with physical and mental inflexibility
- Can't think outside the box and won't take risks
- Sees the world literally. Can be a know it all. Has to learn how to work with limitations
- Can become a slave to work drudgery.

Probable Compatibility Profiles

If you are involved or are a life path number four:

You have to have respect for taking care of others and their loved ones. You need order and organization in your life. If you are unreliable or messy, that won't settle well. You are direct with communication. You have to have complete honesty or the relationship is over. If you are after security, four can give that to you. They need someone who will encourage them and to take risks. They are curious but love learning. If you need somebody to center you, this is the one to do it.

Red Flags:

You are a rule follower. You can cause arguments even while you are telling them you never argue. You can get lost in your work. You can be rigid in your thinking and bossy. You have emotional and family problems that guide most of your life choices. You can easily become slaves to your routine that will cause the relationship to end. At the other end of the spectrum, if a four isn't aligned with their purpose, they won't be able to settle in one location, a job, or anything. They will become a rambler until they finally take responsibility and lay down roots.

5. Freedom Seeker

If your life path number is five, then you are a freedom seeker. Your main purpose is to develop a sense of adventure, fearlessness, and using freedom in whatever you do. You are resilient, fun, curious, vivacious, and an agent of change. You want to experience all the sensual and material world can offer you.

- You are fearless, fun, adventurous, engaging, and exciting
- You are here to experience the world in a very tactile way
- Your mantra is "Don't fence me in!"

Challenges:

- Abandons projects or relationships before giving it a chance or you hang onto until it is completely expired
- Behaviors are excessive
- Can swing from dependence to independence and back again
- Drama King or Queen

Probable Compatibility Profiles

If you are involved with or are a life path number five:

You need freedom! Your mantra is: "Don't fence me in!" You are the life of the party. You are the ultimate adventurer. You love to travel. You are very energetic and attractive. You need to be encouraged to complete one thing before you can move to another. You love to eat great food. You love to dance. Your partner has to be exciting, intelligent, and sensual.

Red Flags:

You need your freedom and space. You will commit to a relationship early on and if they accept it won't last long. You will be fiercely loyal to your partner if you can still have your freedom and independence. You can be a bit scattered and go between complete independence and dependence. Addictions could come into play since you are the master of escape. You need to be prepared for a lot of emotions. On the other side, you might begin to feel afraid instead of fearless and might begin hyperventilating at the mere thought of packing your things. You might become afraid to the point of restricting yourself excessively.

6. The Nurturer

If you are a life path number six, you are a nurturer. Your main purpose is to develop your vision, acceptance, balanced responsibility, and a sense of nurturing. This is the family and home number and will thrive when working with issues that are related to justice, creative arts, or whatever needs a sense of beauty.

- You will have a compassionate heart, supportive nurturer, and natural counselor

- You are often asked to carry everyone's responsibility with friends and family

- You are magnetic, visionary, and an idealist

Challenges:

- Your world is full of should

- You can be a perfectionist and control freak to being a bit self-righteous

- You demand high standards that are impossible for others and yourself

Probable Compatibility Profiles

If you are involved or are a life path number six:

You are the ultimate nurturer and are very responsible. If you are looking for a life partner who will be able, willing, and ready parent, the number six is the one. You are all about family and home. You need to be in control. You will be constantly putting out fires and might feel lost if you aren't responsible for everything. You don't take outside suggestions or criticism well. Make sure you use constructive criticism and praise with a number six life path. They are usually compassionate, heartfelt, and responsible who won't be in it for the long haul.

Red Flags:

You will idealize your partner at the beginning and then get disappointed when reality finally sets in. You can be self-righteous and a perfectionist. You could be a martyr if you gravitate toward destructive tendencies. On the dark side, they can be very critical of the loved ones and very hard to live with. They can be meddlers, enablers, and controllers instead of letting everybody be responsible for themselves. If they are totally off the path, they will be completely irresponsible.

7. The Seeker

If you are a life path number seven you are a seeker. Your main purpose is to create a sense of openness, trust, intuition, data analysis, and a sense of spirituality in everything you do. You are on an internal journey and want to know who you are deep in your core. You want to master the intuitive, spiritual, and analytical nature of life.

- You are complex, intriguing, and mysterious

- You have a very refined mind, ask big questions about life, and is compassionate

- You need to have time alone to unplug and process

Challenges:

- Can be superficial if not connected to their spirituality and a higher sense of purpose

- Works with trust issues

- Has challenges in appearing aloof and over-intellectualizing and being emotionally detached

Probable Compatibility Profiles

If you are involved with or are a life path number seven:

You will always seek the truth about everything, themselves, and the world. You are extremely attractive since they always have an air of mystery to them. They need a spiritual base in their life or they will flounder. If they don't have this base, they could be superficial or have problems with addictions basically anything to stay away from the problem at hand. If you know their base, they will be loving and loyal. They will have trust issues so you have to be sure you are true to them, trustworthy, and honest. They will thrive in nature or when they are near water.

Red Flags:

These people need to have time alone. It won't be anything personal against you. If you give them their downtime without nagging them, they will come back refreshed. They are very intuitive and analytical. They have trust issues and have to work on being open and vulnerable. They want to have a relationship but at the same time, don't.

8. The Powerhouse

If you have a life path number of eight, you are a powerhouse. Your main purpose is to develop a relationship with generosity, authority, control, power, and money in everything you do. You are here to experience the satisfaction that happens with achievement and financial abundance.

- You live a non-linear existence that is full of huge downs and ups
- Life path number eight is the number of money and is a relentless path. You have to master your sense of personal power before you will succeed financially
- You are enticing, care about your image, and is charming

Challenges:

- Heading down the opposite path and become a victim where you have no money or success
- Being opinionated, controlling, and a workaholic
- Being myopically focused on status and money and greedy.

Probable Compatibility Profile

If you are involved with or are a life path number eight:

This life path is all about authority, power, and money. It isn't any wonder that you become attracted to a number eight. These people are outgoing and magnetic. They like to look good and they want their partner to look good, too. Their image is important to them. They can be very romantic and a workaholic. They are intense and charming. You have to be able to support them if they need you to and back off if they don't. They key to their heart is to support them 100% and be able to make them laugh.

Red Flags:

These people can be opinionated and blunt. They are about achievement and be completely focused on their career. They may see their relationships as business terms instead of intimate terms. They are known for being controlling. In the other aspect, a life path number eight who hasn't found their mission might become the victim and become financially impoverished or just don't have any initiative.

9. The Humanitarian

If you are a life path number nine, you are the humanitarian. Your main purpose is to create your sense of integrity, wisdom, creativity, humanitarianism, and spirituality in everything you do. You will be fulfilled if you are serving a humanitarian service and it doesn't matter if it is small or large.

- You are a romantic or an idealist at heart
- You are here to make the world a better place
- You have wonderful charisma, are creative, and will have a lifetime of rewards for their contributions.

Challenges:

- Could be a fanatic about things. Not really a good listener
- Has problems asking for support or help
- Feels like they carry the world on their shoulders

Probable Compatibility Profiles

If you are involved or are a life path number nine:

You will have a ton of charisma. You are very attractive on many levels. You are a natural humanitarian with a giving heart. You are very romantic when talking about relationships. You have to be told what you want, what to do in order to please you, and what you like. You thrive with positive instructions. You never ask for help so you could be having a lot of problems and not even know it. You have to dig deep with this person to know their real feelings.

Red Flags:

These people have a hard time asking for help and can have a lot of family issues. They have a tendency to be fanatics. They have problems letting go. They have a hard time being in the moment so you may not feel like they are listening to you. They have abandonment issues. On the other side of things, they could live in a world that was created by their own resentment and bitterness about their past. They could be a confusing "Rebel Without a Cause" as they are constantly pushing against someone or something.

11. The Old Soul

If you are a life path number 11, you have a master number and are considered to be "an old soul." You have natural intelligence, empathy, increased sensitivity, supernatural abilities, spiritual insight, and high intuition. You have enormous physical and mental power. This is the first master number of the three and the root of all master numbers.

- You have an extreme ability to respect, understand, and empathize with others
- You can work well with pendulums, have prophetic dreams, can see accidents or misfortunes
- You might have the ability of telepathy.

Challenges:

- Highly sensitive and a possible workaholic will spend time working instead of relaxing
- Will put all the responsibility on their shoulders
- Increased probability for addictions like drugs, alcohol, and cigarettes

Probable Compatibility Profiles

If you are involved with or are a life path number 11:

You have the ability to deal with complex problems calmly. You have general knowledge and know a bit about everything. Your best features are an immense ability to see others deeply, sense of order, steadiness, and adaptability, understanding other people's problems, empathy, and respect. You are very creative. You seek and love freedom. You are hard working and will work overtime just to be successful. You will do what you can to make yourself and others feel good. You are a wonderful observer, love animals, nature, and modern technology. You can shut your brain off for a time. You believe in goodness and see things from different perspectives.

They will be very passionate, attractive, sensual, and loyal. They love romance. They put all their effort and energy into their relationships and try to understand everything their partner needs. They know that freedom has its place in relationships.

Red Flags:

These people will spend more time working instead of relaxing. They don't like a lot of openness. They are usually insomniacs. They don't take time for themselves. They put all the responsibility on their shoulders. With all the hypersensitivity and solitude they might develop suicidal tendencies. They create bad habits like drugs, alcohol, and cigarettes.

22. The Master Builder

If you have a life path number of 22, which is another master number, you are the master builder. You are able to turn your dreams into reality but only if they are supported by other numbers in your chart. You have a lot of confidence and aren't interested in idle conversation. You can see "the big picture" and don't like to be near people who don't want to make a change to the world in some way.

- You use your energy because you know who you are

- You attract leaders in your partnerships.

- You take on a lot in life and learn a lot so you can grow and get rid of low vibrations.

Challenges:

- Are usually misunderstood by families and friends

- Sometimes fall into substance abuse if they don't know who they are

- They don't understand why they feel so intense as compared to other people

Probable Compatibility Profiles

If you are involved with or are a life path number 22:

Think how challenging it would be for a person today somebody who wanted to stay home playing games all the time if their nature is to be consuming information and creating projects to help their fellow human beings. It would be a horrible mismatch. If you know yourself, you can use your energy. You probably won't work for anyone else unless you can follow your ideals in that role. Even though you have the practicality of the number four and this makes you organized and reliable. You have the spiritual energy of number 11 that vibrates at higher frequencies.

Red Flags:

If you aren't aware of how different you are, you could become addicted to different substances like drugs, alcohol, and others. You might not understand why your feelings in your mind and heart are so incredibly intense when compared to others who like having a stable life. You might propose large ideas and take huge risks. If their family isn't intuitive, don't look at the big picture, and don't like metaphysics, they might become at odds with their families.

33. The Master Teacher

If you have the life path number of 33, this is also a master number, and you are considered the master teacher. You are the most spiritually evolved. You are very influential since you possess the combination of 11 and 22 which boosts your potential to another level. You find ease in the spiritual aspects of the world. You see your life as an outlet for spiritual energies that aren't easy to master. You are a selfless person.

- You are very knowledgeable
- You check all information before you tell others
- You have a critical mind, many interests, along with logic and creativity

Challenges:

- Wanting to help others is overshadowed by their biases
- Let others be responsible for the actions
- Doesn't like standing out in a crowd

Probable Compatibility Profiles

If you are involved with or are a life path number 33:

You will have a critical mind, many interests, creativity, and logic. People who are attracted to them will pick up universal sympathy and vibrations. They encourage others to understand the essence of being, spiritual creation, and world harmony. They can focus their emotions on spiritual purposes and devote their services to healing and love. They will try to help as many as they possibly can. They really want to help people who aren't able to help themselves. The master teacher will give off the most loving vibration of any number.

Red Flags:

Their desire to help other people gets overshadowed by their own biases and opinions. When they express themselves to their fullest, they will lack ambition and will begin to focus all their ability to uplifting humanity's spirituality.

CHAPTER 14
Balance Number

Everyone reacts a different way when they face challenges in their life. Some might withdraw from a difficult situation to ponder the problem. Other people might withdraw from their emotions so they don't feel anything. Still, others will explode with emotions but let the explosion to quickly pass. While others will linger on their feelings, they hold onto them longer than they should and just can't let them go.

Self-development and maturity will help us learn more effective and new methods of handling the world and all the problems that come with it. Your Balance number in numerology will give you guidance on how you can deal with threatening or difficult situations.

Your balance number gives you information about the hard times you could face within your lifetime. It lets you know how to use your abilities to face the numerous challenges you face in life and the right way to handle these hard times.

This balance number is thought to be only a small influence, well, until your life gets off-balance and you have to rely on this number a lot. If you find yourself going through an emotional turmoil, your balance number will be very important to you. Here is how to find your balance number.

You are probably wondering how to figure out your number. Don't worry, the process is very simple and I'll take you through the entire process. All you need is the full name that was given to you at birth and the following key:

- 1
    - A, J, S
- 2

- B, K, T
- 3
  - C, L, U
- 4
  - D, M, V
- 5
  - E, N, W
- 6
  - F, O, X
- 7
  - G, P, Y
- 8
  - H, Q, Z
- 9
  - I, R

To find your balance number, you will add the numerical value to your initials. Here's an example: let's use the name Jessie Matilda Edwards: her initials are J, M, and E. Their numerical values are 1, 4, and 5. To calculate their balance number you simply add 1+4+5=10, which will reduce down to 1. Jessie has a balanced number of 1. You have to reduce any double-digit number into a single digit when figuring out your balance number and this includes Master numbers.

Balance Number Meanings

Ones: People who have the number one will have the capability and confidence to handle situations effectively. You have to give value to other people's points of view, also. Having this attitude could help you in the long run. You won't ask anyone to help you because of your huge ego. You can be extremely stubborn and aggressive.

When you can overcome these drawbacks, you will be able to have success in all walks of life. You need to use your sense of awareness. You have the ability to ask other people for help if you need to. You can react with capability and confidence in any situation. You have strength and courage to win this way but another person's advice might be helpful, too. Stay away from being obstinate.

You need to have a good balance of creativity and courage. You draw strength from within yourself but when you share your problems with family and friends it can help you, too. You like being a loner when facing problems. This makes you more isolated.

You need to be open to getting advice from others. This widens your views about the problem and can give you new information that you can figure out how to approach the problem. If you get the number one during a reading, you need to exercise your courage, creativity, and strength to win your war.

Twos: People who have the number two let other people lead and influence than when times get hard. You don't have the fortitude and confidence that you need to face a hard situation. You don't have any nerves in hard times. You need to learn how to be reflective, composed and calm so you can find a decent way to solve the problem.

Rather than letting other people influence you, you have to give your inner instincts value, too. You have to take a balanced approach when handling situations. Your approach needs to more tactful. You need to absorb your courage so you can finish the task at hand. You shouldn't be afraid of anyone.

Being emotional isn't going to help you at all. Make sure other people's opinions don't influence you. Remain calm during these situations. Harmony and balance are needed to win.

When you have a balanced number of two, you have to work to diffuse the tension and use your talents to find a solution that works for everyone. You will have a compromising nature.

Try your best not to panic and blow things out of proportion. You need to work harmoniously and be balanced so you can handle any problem that comes your way. You can be a peacemaker during conflicts.

Threes: People who have the number three are talkative. You have to be articulate so you can express your opinions and views more effectively to people. You should be tactful and use any means available to you and use them in the best way so you can be successful.

During difficult situations, you might lose confidence in yourself. You get confused and nervous and this makes it harder for you. You need to apply simple solutions so you don't mess things up. You need to learn to express your opinions and views clearly.

You need to control your tongue at times. You need to learn to listen better. You have to use all the best resources to finish your task. You need to be confident and optimistic to achieve your goals. Your approach needs to be lighthearted when solving problems.

When you have a balanced number of three in a reading, try to work in groups to find a mutually satisfying solution. You possess a natural charm. Use this charm to influence your situations. You can be extremely emotional when you face problems. You need to control this and solve the problem objectively. You become attached to the solution you are looking for. This makes it hard for you to see if the outcome will help everyone involved.

Fours: People who have the number four fail to see situations, are emotional, and solve their problems practically. You won't compromise and are conventional. You possess preconceived ideas about certain things and need to learn how to look at situations completely and come to a conclusion after you have thought about all the cons and pros.

You need to trust others and show your compassion and understanding. You need to learn how to be realistic and practical when solving problems because when you are emotional, it isn't going to help you. Try to stay away from having fixed thoughts about problems and try not to be too stubborn. You need to be more compromising.

You should show understanding and love for everyone. You need to deal with problems that are emotionally charged lightheartedly. You need to work on controlling your anger and practice some self-discipline. Take a look at the big picture instead of getting confused in the details.

If you have a balanced number four, you need to show justice by showing understanding, compassion, and forgiveness to others. You will be able to tackle confrontations by putting yourself in their shoes.

Fives: People who have number five, have conventional and rigid viewpoints. You live conventionally. You don't like changing and adapting to new conditions. You like using tried and true methods to deal with situations.

You should be trendier and try new innovative ways to solve problems. If you can't keep up with the times you will fall behind. If you face hard situations, you will get nervous and try to stay away from the situation.

If you use all of your abilities, you will find success in every challenging situation in your life. You need to be adaptable and flexible to changes and open your mind by exploring new approaches and thoughts. Always enjoy the little things in life.

You need to deal with your problems instead of avoiding them and making excuses. If you can put your mind to it, you will find a solution. Stay focused on the problem. You have a tendency to indulge in drugs, alcohol, and junk food. You can find a creative solution to all situations when you begin to focus.

Sixes: People who have the number six, you don't have any confidence in your abilities even though you possess great qualities. You ask other people for suggestions to help solve problems. You need to know what you are capable of and give your and other people's judgments value.

You need to have a balanced approach to life. You don't take responsibility for any mistakes you make. You always blame others. This gives people a negative impression of you. You need to be more mature, responsible, and independent if you want to be loved and respected by everyone.

You need to realize and understand that honesty will always be the best policy. You need to use this when you are dealing with conflict. Try to confront the situation by yourself instead of depending on others. When you take responsibility, it will make you more self-reliant and confident. You have to learn how to forgive others for their mistakes rather than punishing them. You are loving in nature and are loved by everyone.

You have to understand that your strength is understanding people and the conflict. You aren't aware of this and rely too much on your family and friends to give you comfort rather than handling the situation responsibly and directly.

When you are confronted with a difficult situation, you will normally turn to someone else's support and suggestions. You have to be more responsible. You have to help yourself to solve different problems

Sevens: People who have this number are very emotional and deal with every situation emotionally. You have to realize that life isn't a bed of roses and there is going to be bad and good times every now and then.

Remember to keep cool and look at the situation analytically so it gets easier to solve the problem. You have to fight your own battles. You need to know how to use your analytical mind to solve any problem.

Don't get emotional about small problems because this won't solve the problem. Rather than running away, confront the problem and figure out a solution. You have to be in control of your emotions and learn to think logically.

If you are faced with a difficult situation, you will retreat into yourself to get away from it. You have to realize your mind's analytical abilities are enough to give you all the insight to solve every problem, and to find a path to the solution.

You have to put in an effort when finding and confronting solutions for any issue you are facing by staying calm and unemotional. You have a tendency to be swamped in the emotions of the problem. These will dominate your mind and keeps you from using your intelligence to find the answer. You need to stay away from emotions when looking for the answer. You need to learn how to find a solution for everyone's well being.

Eights: People who have the number eight don't have any patience. You try to complete and do things as quickly as possible no matter the cost. You have to learn to be organized and systematic. When you are facing a problem, you get nervous and confused and just make the problem worse. You have to compromise with your integrity and honesty.

You might try to solve the problem by using ruthless and manipulative tactics. You have to know that there is a place and time for everything. This means you have to deal with things at a particular time and when you lose your patience, it isn't going to help you. If you use shortcuts when solving problems, it isn't the easy way and might cause problems in the future.

You need more stability and balance. Use your power in a balanced way, even though you have a tendency to use it in a manipulative way instead of confronting it properly.

Use your powers nobly for things such as accepting responsibility to the situation and finding a good solution for the problem. You have a lot of creative and artistic talent. You have the ability to find the answer to just about any problem. You shouldn't try to be so dominating and on your opinion on others. You should include their ideas and concerns when finding the solution.

Nines: People who have the number nine, are understanding and compassionate. You do tend to be aloof. You like your solitude but will always be there to help and support other people when they are having a hard time. People often misunderstand you because of your introverted nature. You think you are self-centered and arrogant.

You have to be open and show your true feelings to let people understand the real you. You have to show patience and compassion to solve problems. You need to understand that you can do a lot of things with love. Learn to be involved with others and their problems rather than being standoffish.

You need to take an interest in what concerns others. This allows you to find solutions. You have an understanding nature. You are able to understand situations and things on a broader level.

You have a tendency to retreat into acting standoffish where you think you are an aristocrat and above everyone else. You will only find solutions when you are realistic and practical. You receive by giving to others.

CHAPTER 15
Double-Digit Number

Your birth information and name can tell you what number will dominate your life. These numbers will be able to tell you much about your personality and future. There are two types of numbers: "cardinal" or single-digit and double-digit numbers. To go in depth with your own numero-identity, we have to look at everything.

Double-digits are a bit trickier to understand. You have to know how to calculate specific number like a birth date or expression number can seem complex but the process is very simple. We are going to explore the next level in numerology that involves tracing the meaning back to the number's roots or back to the double-digit number. These meanings can be complex but by using this guide you will have all the tools you need to explore double-digits.

Double Versus Single

Most people understand the difference between double and single digit numbers. As stated above, a single digit number is also called "cardinal" numbers and are the numbers one through nine. Double digits have two numbers like the number 11. Before you can start exploring numerology with double digits, you need to grasp the basics of numerology first. This means you need to understand numbers and how to reduce.

If you don't understand these steps if is going to be very difficult to understand and double-digit meanings. When studying numerology, it involves precise calculations and if you don't understand even one step, like just enough to lead to an incorrect number will be enough to give you a completely incorrect reading.

Reducing and Cardinal Numbers

Let's talk about cardinal numbers and how to reduce. A cardinal number is any single digit number that can reflect the deepest meaning of what you are investigating. The main problem comes from when you do the calculations; we leave the single digits behind early.

If you use your sun number as an example, it will be calculated using your birthday and month. When you combine the two together, you get your sun number. For this example, if you were born after the ninth in any month or after August you total should be above nine.

Let's say you were born August 15th. You could calculate this by adding the numbers 8 and 15 and this will give you 23. It is easy to see that 23 isn't a single digit number so you can't investigate your sun number if they only range from one to nine. This is when you have to reduce. Reducing is very easy as you take that double-digit number and turn it into a single digit number. You can easily do this by adding the two digits together. For example, the 23 would reduce down to five.

A five that comes from the number two and three will have more characteristics from the numbers two and three. If the five came from a one and four, it would have characteristics from the one and four. The number five could describe a wide range of personality traits; there are various types of fives. Due to this, many numerologists will write out single numbers that include the double-digit numbers that they came from such as 15/6, 25/7, 11/2.

Double-Digit Numerology

Let's focus our attention on double-digit numbers. They are usually overshadowed by single numbers that they add up to. You might hear the number seven represents a person who is withdrawn. Somebody might be a seven because they have a 25 in their chart will be less withdrawn that a person who is a seven that comes from a 16.

How does this relate to spiritual meanings of double number? When specific core numbers could be obtained by reducing, like sum numbers, this isn't going to always be the case. Some calculations might involve reducing but we can't forget the original numbers.

This gives the double-digit number a new area to explore for people who are new to numerology. It can be confusing. If we can break the process down little by little, then you will start to understand. Think about looking for information about a person and one number you can work with is 49.

You can't look at 49 by itself without reducing it down to the core number: 4+9=13, 1+3=4. You would get a core number of four but what about the double numbers? You have two double numbers you can work with and there are two things you have to think about before you look at the other meanings.

The Root Number

If you stay with the above example, you have three numbers in total. You have the original number of 49, you have the reduced number of 13 and the core number of four.

Looking at the core number is easy since there are only nine to pick from but what do you do with the double numbers? Which one do you look at?

When you try to explore the reduced meanings of double digits, you can only go back as far as the numbers will allow. If you have a number 257, you will reduce it to 14 and then to five. You can only work with the numbers 14 and five.

In the other example of 49, you would focus on the number 49 and think about the reduced number of 13 in passing. Looking at the roots of any number will give you a different perspective.

If you have the number 23 and the number 14, they will both reduce down to five. Does this mean that both numbers are the same? No, they won't. The 23's reduced number of five will have roots in the two and seven while the 14's five will have roots in the one and four.

What Does All This Mean?

It means that for any number that was reduced from a double number, you can look at many numbers to expand their meaning.

If your original number was 23, you can explore the number five while also looking at the numbers two and three.

This allows you to have a more detailed understanding of any number because it won't make sense if each number can be broken down one of nine meanings. Hopefully, you have a better understanding of double-digit numbers.

Meanings of Double-Digit Numbers

As a general rule, numbers that can be divided by ten will strengthen the characteristics of the single digit numbers. Ten is a high octave one. 40 has a high octave of four. 70 will have a high octave of seven.

Here are the double-digit numbers beginning at ten and going all the way to 99 and what they mean:

10. The number 10 enhances all the qualities of one. These people will be powerful leaders. They are streamlined for success. They are sharply focused. They can be ruthless when pursuing their goals. They have the potential to become dominating tyrants.

11. The number 11 is a "master number". These people will be very intuitive and some might be psychics. This "master number" can be a channel between the conscious and subconscious mind. They are very highly charged and can sometimes be neurotic.

12. People who have the number 12 will be unconventional. They are very individualistic meaning they like being by themselves. Most are very creative. They will always rely on themselves more than they would a group. They can be a tab selfish and are always a bit irresponsible. They don't manage time well and are very inefficient.

13. The number 13 is a called a "Karmic Debt number." These people work very hard but don't show any progress. This number is hard but very rewarding if enough effort is given. They are down-to-earth people who always stay grounded. They don't have a sense of humor. They can be rigid but are

very trustworthy and reliable. They can express their feelings and ideas better than many fours.

14. The number 14 is another "Karmic Debt number. These people have a need for adventure and change that usually gets in the way of progress. They don't like commitments. They have very little focus. This number could get you into trouble if you don't consciously exercise discipline. Every five needs to guard themselves against indulging but when they are based on a 14, a selfish side pops up that will amplify their lack of control.

15. People who have the number 15 will be very tolerant. They forgive easily and are very loving. They are very strong, dynamic, successful, and responsible. People who are 15s will have fewer constraints that normal sixes and like to enjoy adventure and travel. They are loyal to a fault and very family oriented. They are unconventional and like their privacy.

16. The number 16 is another "Karmic Debt number". These people have had a difficult time growing up. They have a lot of potential for self-knowledge and spiritual growth. This number is connected to "the fallen tower" in tarot. These people can be a tad self-destructive but they represent the Phoenix rising from its ashes. This is the most influential of the Karmic numbers. It can bring wisdom through hardships as you age.

17. People who have the number 17 are balanced. They are faithful in their spiritual growth. They will either be extremely wealthy or bankrupt. They will have inner struggles to stay true to the moral values and spirituality all while dedicating themselves to materialistic things. This is the most conflicting number.

18. People who have the number 18 will be involved in businesses all over the world. They will be in discord between selfishness and idealism. They won't have any efforts spiritually. If you are an 18, you will benefit from traveling and reading.

19. The number 19 is another "Karmic Debt number." These people will be very confident, self-reliant, individualistic, and strong. This "Karmic Debt number could bring you alienation and loneliness because you don't have support from other people. They will have leadership qualities but are at times a bit bullish.

20. People who have the number 20 can't handle criticism. They are very intuitive but too sensitive. They have many emotional problems and are very unstable. They show cowardice and weakness if challenged but can also be survivors and very resilient.

21. People who have the number 21 are similar to 12 as they are unconventional, individualistic, and creative. They will rely on themselves and are a bit irresponsible. They can't manage their time and are inefficient. A number three that is based on 21 can be more cooperative, sensitive, and intuitive. They will play better with other people.

22. The number 22 is another "Master number." These people are obsessive, demanding. They can push you to your edge. They can make a lot of progress if they try. They have to devote themselves to something that is larger than life.

23. People who have the number 23 like to promote causes. They will fight for their freedom and loves people. On the flip side, they can often be unrealistic and quitters. They are more creative than other fives.

24. People who have the number 24 likes playing percussion instruments but almost any instrument will do. They are sixes based on 24 and they like to comfort and counsel others. They might have been in many relationships and possibly divorces. They need a stable, solid environment. They tend to gossip too much.

25. People who have the number 25 are usually spiritual leaders. They like working in groups. This is the opposite of most sevens. They have difficulty sharing their feelings and can be a bit too serious. They have a restless streak and are rather self-indulgent.

26. People who have the number 26 are excellent in management and business. They work well with others and are good at strategies. They can be workaholics. But in their personal lives, they are quite the opposite. They are usually an over domineering parent, lazy and disorganized.

27. People who have the number 27 are usually successful, Some will be artists but they like volunteering and counseling others. These people usually inherit their money or it comes from unearned or unexpected sources. The number nine is a little judgmental or prejudiced, 27 can be narrow-minded and rigid.

28. People who have the number 28 might think they are the same as a ten but they will have more tolerance and compassion. They also possess more determination and ambition. The number 28 is a warrior's number.

29. People who have the number 29 are the same as number 11. These people might be a bit more cynical, less social, and more serious.

30. People who have the number 30 are creative and communicate well. This number is a high octave three. They will possess a wonderful sense of humor. They are normally warm and jovial but a bit superficial. They don't have any staying power and get distracted easily.

31. People who have the number 31 will be more fun loving and more of an extrovert than most other fours. They can be more creative and unfaithful to their partners.

32. People who have the number 32 can look back at 23 which is unrealistic, a quitter promotes causes, and fights for their freedom. Number 32 is more sensitive. They are moodier and won't commit to anything and this includes relationships.

33. The number 33 is another "Master number." They can reach high levels of wisdom and consciousness. Their ultimate potential is to teach teachers. They comfort others. They are idealists and often self-sacrifice. When they don't live up to

their potential, they tend to be codependent. They like bending the truth and are arrogant.

34. People who have the number 34 can expend a lot of effort for a long amount of time. They are very intelligent and could attain spiritual greatness. These people are intellectual warriors and enjoy taking the path less followed. They love to upset the status quo. They have a tendency to be stubborn and prideful.

35. People who have the number 35 are usually business advisers, inventors, creative in business, or good at designing gadgets. They are fairly social but won't work well with other people. They are too independent and work better as a freelancer.

36. People who have the number 36 are sometimes thought of as geniuses. They are extremely creative. They can be aloof, inhibited, and self-conscious. Even though it has a three at the first digit, they will have a hard time expressing their feelings and thoughts. They make up for it with math or visual arts.

37. People who have the number 37 have wonderful imaginations, very individualistic, scholars, and love to read. They will read anything they can get their hands on. They are sometimes disorganized.

38. The number 38 is similar to the number 11. They will be more realistic but tend to be sticks in the mud. They are great in business but don't work well with people. They are a little bit insecure and easily offended.

39. People who have the number 39 love functional art. They are often dancing or acting. They don't like being separated from others and has a hard time with rejection.

40. The number 40 is a high octave four. People who possess this number are very organized, methodical, and systematic. They have a high probability of success in almost all they do but does guard themselves against get-rich schemes. They

can be very critical of others. They are sometimes judgmental and intolerant.

41. People who have the number 41 have the ability to direct their energies into many projects at the same time and are successful at doing it. They can be a bit compulsive and they have to guard against being self-indulgent. A person who is a negative 41 can be selfish, won't have a sense of humor and could easily turn into a criminal.

42. People who have the number 42 usually aspire to be in politics. They can be an administrator usually in government. They have a tendency to be insensitive but they need a predictable and stable environment. They could end up with phobias or OCD.

43. People who have the number 43 are usually very spiritual and sometimes eccentric. This is the hermit's number. Some people will have feelings of inferiority, easily frustrated, concentrates well, and are perfectionists. They love to push conspiracy theories and upset the status quo but are very intelligent. They can be cynical and stubborn.

44. People who have the number 44 have a good head for business. They would also do well in the military. They are doers and visionaries. They have excellent potential. If the person is a negative 44, they can be inflexible and boring.

45. People who have the number 45 are usually involved with international institutes or banking. They struggle to be comfortable with themselves and could be a bit cynical.

46. People who have the number 46 will have perseverance, drive, and leadership. They will always be confident and prepared. They are trustworthy but can be rude and tactless. They have a tendency to be bullies.

47. The number 47 is similar to the number 11. They will have an inner struggle between being spiritual (7), down to earth (4), and practical. When the balance has been achieved, they will be a counselor or prophet.

48. People who have the number 48 are planners and visionaries. They sometimes get lost in dreams that aren't real.

49. The number 49 is similar to the number 13. People are often caretakers that help others. They will be problem solvers. They want to be friends or heroes to everybody.

50. The number is a high octave five. These people love their freedom and are very versatile. They are open to new ideas and are willing to take chances. They sometimes have sexual hang-ups.

51. The number 51 is similar to 15. People who have this number are more aggressive and independent.

52. The number 52 is similar to 25 but people are more creative, intuitive, and sensitive.

53. The number 53 is similar to 35 but is more business oriented, creative, and verbal.

54. The number 54 is similar to 45 but it isn't as disciplined and organized. They will have a hard time finishing projects they have started. They are usually dreamers and are very idealistic.

55. People who have the number 55 usually love to travel and love their freedom. They are social but can be lonely and selfish. They will be successful in sales.

56. People who have the number 56 have a hard combination. They represent extreme sensitivity and have to balance their desire for freedom with an equal desire for family. Reference back to number 11.

57. People who have the number 57 will be inventive and intelligent. They possess wisdom later in life. They are unconventional and creative.

58. People who have the number 58 will work hard and are usually successful. They will recognize opportunities and

are able to make decisions quickly. They are opinionated and dogmatic.

59. People who have the number 59 are very convincing and persuasive. They are found to be successful lawyers and fundraisers. They bring the ability to be comfortable with all people in all walks of life and cultures.

60. People who have the number 60 are responsible, caring, and loving. They are sometimes subservient.

61. People who have the number 61 will have a hard time in relationships of love. They have a strong need for friends and family. They are secretive and demanding. They usually look for jobs in the Secret Service, law officers, or researchers.

62. The number 62 is similar to the number 26. People with this number won't be as sensitive. They are excellent caretakers. People who have this number work great in the medical field.

63. The number 63 is similar to 36. They aren't as outgoing but can be sexually promiscuous.

64. The number 64 is similar to 46 but is more creative and not as organized.

65. The number 65 is similar to 56 but they need to balance their domestic commitments and their freedom. This number can lead to becoming a criminal.

66. People who have the number 66 will have financial ups and downs but are generous to a fault. They are very loving and loyal. They are usually successful in spite of themselves.

67. People who have the number 67 will merge creativity with analytical intelligence. These people are usually mathematicians or inventors. They will usually have this number on their chart but behind another core number.

68. People who have the number 68 have a good head for business. They are usually insensitive but very loyal. They will have a great sense of humor.

69. People who have the number 69 are self-sacrificing. There aren't any other numbers that are as self-sacrificing as this one. Environmentalists and political activists usually have this number just like teachers, nurses, and doctors. These people will be very creative.

70. People who have the number 70 are usually hermits. They like to be alone but seek the truth. They often get caught up in seeking knowledge to the extent that they lose touch with the world around them. They are highly original and intelligence. They are always eccentric.

71. The number 71 is similar to the number 17 but they are usually loners and won't be as authoritative.

72. The number 72 is similar to the number 27. These people are great at conversations and love to read.

73. The number 73 is similar to the number 37. These people like to work by themselves and are independent. They are very demanding in their relationships.

74. The number 74 is similar to the numbers 11 and 47. These people will sometimes have intense dreams and premonitions. They can sometimes develop eating disorders.

75. The number 75 is similar to 57 but they aren't as creative and more analytical.

76. The number 76 is similar to 67. These people are usually involved with organizations or management. They can turn ideas into realities. This number could cause religious fanaticism and dogmatism.

77. The number 77 just like all double-digit number who have identical digits, it is a power number but not a Master number. People who have this number are very intelligent

and will always be spiritual. They won't take anything for granted. They will be skeptical and are usually found in libraries or on spiritual retreats. They won't be found in places of worships or belonging to any organized religion. As a person ages, this number will be wisdom. The number behind 77 is 14 and this adds independence and individuality along with a stubborn streak. The cardinal number that 77 reduces down to is five and this brings personality, love of adventure and freedom. Fives are tolerant, adaptable, and flexible.

78. People who have the number 78 will always struggle between material and spiritual. They will make and lose many fortunes.

79. People who have the number 79 are usually spiritual and political leaders. They have concern for mankind but could be self-righteous and ruthless.

80. People who have the number 80 usually do well in business. They are usually in the military and top management rather than entrepreneurs because they lack independence. They are normally extroverts.

81. The number 81 is similar to 18 but they are more money-oriented. They don't have any spiritual understanding. They could have a bit of a violent streak.

82. The number 82 is similar to 28 but will have a lot of courage and leadership. They are always survivors. They usually don't have any stability in their marriages. Most people who have this number won't get married or will be married many times.

83. The number 83 is similar to the number 38 but will be more business oriented and won't be as vulnerable and sensitive.

84. The number 84 is similar to the number 48 but are less organized and more of a visionary.

85. The number 85 is similar to 58 but is more masculine and can be bullish

86. The number 86 is similar to 68 but is more self-oriented. They can be a bit self-indulgent and irresponsible.

87. The number 87 is similar to 78 but they are more practical and will handle money a lot better. They will struggle between material and spiritual things.

88. People who have the number 88 are full of contradictions. They are great in business but not for relationships. They are very insensitive.

89. People who have the number 89 will be aristocrats. They will be the women or men of the world. They will travel a lot. They don't like to be alone, even for short amounts of time.

90. People who have the number 90 will be humble and self-sacrificing. They will be super religious but always inspiring and positive in nature. People who have this number are aloof but respected and loved by many.

91. People who have the number 91 will always be successful, especially if they are creative. They don't do well handling money. They are usually opinionated and eccentric.

92. The number 92 is similar to number 11 they have a lot of concerns for mankind.

93. The number 93 is similar to 39. They are creative, especially in landscaping and architecture. They have a hard time with commitment.

94. The number 94 is similar to 49. They will be humanitarians. They aren't comfortable traveling and don't like change.

95. The number 95 is similar to 59. They are humanitarians but are dreamers and impractical. They love change and travel.

96. The number 96 is similar to 69. They are loving and self-sacrificing in nature. They focus more on their community, friends, and family.

97. The number 97 is similar to 79 but they are more sensitive. They work quietly and love to read.

98. The number 98 is similar to 89 but the idealism is a bit indifferent. They have a hard time showing emotions. Other people can't understand them too well.

99. People who have this number are artistic geniuses. They are usually misunderstood and are frequently victims of gossip. They often bring possessiveness and jealousy to their relationships.

CONCLUSION

Thank for making it through to the end of *Numerology Easy Guide for Beginners*, I hope it was informative and able to provide you with all of the tools you need for your numerology journey.

The next steps should be using some of the information you have learned. Try out the techniques and see what you can learn about your numbers. This can be helpful in many different areas of your life. Plus, it's just plain fun to do.

Finally, if you found this book useful in any way, a review on Amazon is always appreciated!

DESCRIPTION

If you are looking for new insights into your life, then you may find numerology helpful.

Numerology, which is simply the study of numbers, is an ancient tool used to learn more about a person. Each number involved in a numerology reading explains a different aspect about a person, and all it uses are simple things like their name and birth date.

Numerology also has connections with other metaphysical tools, such as astrology and tarot. This book will cover all of this and more. You will learn:

- What numerology is
- How to create your birth chart
- The meanings of numerology numbers
- What master numbers are
- What numbers can tell about you
- And much more

The best thing about numerology is that it is really easy to learn. Once you have figured out the equation for the different numbers, you can provide anybody with a numerology reading. It's a simple way to get a little insight into your life.

If you are looking to learn a new skill, or if you just want to learn something fun, this book is for you. Numerology is fun and easy, so get this book today.

www.ingramcontent.com/pod-product-compliance
Lightning Source LLC
Chambersburg PA
CBHW071502070526
44578CB00001B/414